ECONOMIC ISSUES, PROBLEMS AND PERSPECTIVES

THE FEDERAL RESERVE: FUNCTIONS AND POLICIES

ECONOMIC ISSUES, PROBLEMS AND PERSPECTIVES

Additional books in this series can be found on Nova's website under the Series tab.

Additional E-books in this series can be found on Nova's website under the E-books tab.

AMERICA IN THE 21ST CENTURY: POLITICAL AND ECONOMIC ISSUES

Additional books in this series can be found on Nova's website under the Series tab.

Additional E-books in this series can be found on Nova's website under the E-books tab.

ECONOMIC ISSUES, PROBLEMS AND PERSPECTIVES

THE FEDERAL RESERVE: FUNCTIONS AND POLICIES

John P. Ranchett
EDITOR

Nova Science Publishers, Inc.
New York

Copyright © 2011 by Nova Science Publishers, Inc.

All rights reserved. No part of this book may be reproduced, stored in a retrieval system or transmitted in any form or by any means: electronic, electrostatic, magnetic, tape, mechanical photocopying, recording or otherwise without the written permission of the Publisher.

For permission to use material from this book please contact us:
Telephone 631-231-7269; Fax 631-231-8175
Web Site: http://www.novapublishers.com

NOTICE TO THE READER

The Publisher has taken reasonable care in the preparation of this book, but makes no expressed or implied warranty of any kind and assumes no responsibility for any errors or omissions. No liability is assumed for incidental or consequential damages in connection with or arising out of information contained in this book. The Publisher shall not be liable for any special, consequential, or exemplary damages resulting, in whole or in part, from the readers' use of, or reliance upon, this material. Any parts of this book based on government reports are so indicated and copyright is claimed for those parts to the extent applicable to compilations of such works.

Independent verification should be sought for any data, advice or recommendations contained in this book. In addition, no responsibility is assumed by the publisher for any injury and/or damage to persons or property arising from any methods, products, instructions, ideas or otherwise contained in this publication.

This publication is designed to provide accurate and authoritative information with regard to the subject matter covered herein. It is sold with the clear understanding that the Publisher is not engaged in rendering legal or any other professional services. If legal or any other expert assistance is required, the services of a competent person should be sought. FROM A DECLARATION OF PARTICIPANTS JOINTLY ADOPTED BY A COMMITTEE OF THE AMERICAN BAR ASSOCIATION AND A COMMITTEE OF PUBLISHERS.

Additional color graphics may be available in the e-book version of this book.

Library of Congress Cataloging-in-Publication Data

The Federal Reserve : functions and policies / editor, John P. Ranchett.
  p. cm.
  Includes index.
  ISBN 978-1-62100-528-5 (hardcover)
  1. Board of Governors of the Federal Reserve System (U.S.). 2. Federal Reserve banks.
  3. B Monetary policy--United States. 4. United States--Economic policy. I. Ranchett, John P.
  HG2565.F42 2011
  332.1'10973--dc23
                                                                            2011035505

Published by Nova Science Publishers, Inc. ✢ *New York*

CONTENTS

Preface		vii
Chapter 1	Structure and Functions of the Federal Reserve System *Pauline Smale*	1
Chapter 2	Monetary Policy and the Federal Reserve: Current Policy and Conditions *Marc Labonte and Joseph R. McCormack*	11
Chapter 3	Economics of Federal Reserve Independence *Marc Labonte*	33
Chapter 4	Changing the Federal Reserve's Mandate: An Economic Analysis *Marc Labonte*	55
Chapter 5	Inflation: Core vs. Headline *Marc Labonte*	85
Chapter 6	Quantitative Easing and the Growth in the Federal Reserve's Balance Sheet *Marc Labonte*	93

Chapter 7	Remarks by Ben S. Bernanke, Chairman, Board of Governors of the Federal Reserve System, at the Federal Reserve Bank of Chicago, 47th Annual Conference on Bank Structure and Competition, Hearing on "Implementing a Macroprudential Approach to Supervision and Regulation"	121
Index		133

PREFACE

In 1913, Congress created the Federal Reserve System to serve as the central bank for the United States. The Federal Reserve formulates the nation's monetary policy, supervises and regulates banks, and provides a variety of financial services to depository financial institutions and the federal government. The system comprises three major components: the Board of Governors, a network of 12 Federal Reserve Banks and member banks. Congress created the Federal Reserve as an independent agency to enable the central bank to carry out its responsibilities protected from excessive political and private pressures. At the same time, by law and practice, the Federal Reserve is accountable to Congress. This book examines the structure and operations of the major components of the Federal Reserve System and provides an overview of congressional oversight activities with a focus on the Dodd-Frank Wall Street Reform and Consumer Protection Act.

Chapter 1- In 1913, Congress created the Federal Reserve System to serve as the central bank for the United States. The Federal Reserve formulates the nation's monetary policy, supervises and regulates banks, and provides a variety of financial services to depository financial institutions and the federal government. The system comprises three major components: the Board of Governors, a network of 12 Federal Reserve Banks, and member banks.

Chapter 2- The Federal Reserve (Fed) defines monetary policy as the actions it undertakes to influence the availability and cost of money and credit. Since the expectations of market participants play an important role in determining prices and growth, monetary policy can also be defined to include the directives, policies, statements, and actions of the Fed that influence how the future is perceived. In addition, the Fed acts as a "lender of last resort" to the nation's financial system, meaning that it ensures continued smooth functioning of financial intermediation by providing financial markets with adequate liquidity. This role has become of great importance following the onset of the recent financial crisis.

Chapter 3- The Federal Reserve System (Fed) is charged with responsibility for making U.S. monetary policy. Quasi-public in structure, overseen by a Board of Governors whose members are appointed to serve long terms, and reliant on its own source of funding, the Fed possesses a degree of independence that some argue is inimical to the spirit of democracy. Although this argument (and refutations of it) may be political or constitutional in nature, it is also rooted in certain notions about macroeconomic policy.

Chapter 4- The Federal Reserve's (Fed's) current statutory mandate calls for it to "promote effectively the goals of maximum employment, stable prices, and moderate long-term interest rates." Some economists have argued that the current mandate should be replaced with a single mandate of price stability. Often the proposal for a single mandate is paired with a more specific proposal that the Fed should adopt an inflation target. Under an inflation target, the goal of monetary policy would be to achieve an explicit, numerical target or range for some measure of price inflation. Inflation targets could be required by Congress or voluntarily adopted by the Fed as a way to pursue price stability, or a single mandate could be adopted without an inflation target. Alternatively, an inflation target could be adopted under the current mandate.

Chapter 5- Inflation measures the rate of change in all prices. Maintaining low and stable inflation is one of the primary goals of macroeconomic policy. But how should inflation be measured? Policymakers, particularly at the Federal Reserve, often refer to *core* inflation in their policy decisions. Core inflation is commonly defined as a measure of inflation that omits changes in food and energy prices. Some policymakers prefer to use core inflation to predict future overall inflation because food and energy price volatility makes it difficult to discern trends from the overall inflation rate. A drawback of an over-reliance on core inflation, however, is that an extended period of rapidly rising food or energy prices could cause all other prices to accelerate. A focus on core may cause policymakers to fail to react to such a rise in inflation until it is too late. This scenario may have occurred recently. Many economists are concerned that rapid increases in food and energy prices are now pushing overall inflation to uncomfortably high levels. Furthermore, several studies have failed to find core inflation to be a good forecaster of future inflation, casting doubt on the very rationale for relying on it.

Chapter 6- On November 3, 2010, the Federal Reserve (Fed) announced that it would purchase an additional $600 billion of Treasury securities, an action that has popularly been dubbed quantitative easing or "QE2." This announcement followed purchases since March 2009 of $300 billion of Treasury securities, $175 billion of agency debt, and $1.25 trillion of agency mortgage-backed securities (MBS). (The agency debt and MBS were primarily issued by Fannie Mae and Freddie Mac.) This report defines quantitative easing as actions to further stimulate the economy through growth in the Fed's balance sheet once the federal funds rate has reached the "zero bound."

Chapter 7- The recent financial crisis revealed critical gaps and weaknesses in the U.S. financial system and the financial regulatory framework. The Congress and the Administration last year provided a roadmap for addressing many of these problems, in the form of the Dodd-Frank Wall Street Reform and Consumer Protection Act (Dodd-Frank Act)-- the topic of this year's conference.

Legislative reforms in any complex area always face the risk of fighting the last war, responding to the causes of the last crisis without sufficient attention to where new problems may arise. To their credit, the authors of the Dodd-Frank Act attempted to reduce this risk by building in a number of features aimed at helping our system of financial oversight adapt over time to changes in the financial environment. Notably, a central element of the legislation is the requirement that the Federal Reserve and other financial regulatory agencies adopt a so-called macroprudential approach--that is, an approach that supplements traditional supervision and regulation of individual firms or markets with explicit consideration of threats to the stability of the financial system as a whole. The act also created a new Financial Stability Oversight Council, whose membership comprises a diverse group of federal and state financial regulators, to coordinate the government's efforts to identify and respond to systemic risks.

In: The Federal Reserve
Editor: John P. Ranchett

ISBN: 978-1-62100-528-5
© 2011 Nova Science Publishers, Inc.

Chapter 1

STRUCTURE AND FUNCTIONS OF THE FEDERAL RESERVE SYSTEM[*]

Pauline Smale

SUMMARY

In 1913, Congress created the Federal Reserve System to serve as the central bank for the United States. The Federal Reserve formulates the nation's monetary policy, supervises and regulates banks, and provides a variety of financial services to depository financial institutions and the federal government. The system comprises three major components: the Board of Governors, a network of 12 Federal Reserve Banks, and member banks.

Congress created the Federal Reserve as an independent agency to enable the central bank to carry out its responsibilities protected from excessive political and private pressures. At the same time, by law and practice, the Federal Reserve is accountable to Congress. The seven members of the board are appointed by the President with the advice and consent of the Senate. Congress routinely monitors the Federal Reserve System through formal and informal oversight activities.

This report examines the structure and operations of the major components of the Federal Reserve System and provides an overview of

---

[*] This is an edited, reformatted and augmented version of a Congressional Research Service publication, CRS Report for Congress RS20826, from www.crs.gov, dated November 10, 2010.

congressional oversight activities. The report identifies the provisions of P.L. 111-203 (the Dodd-Frank Wall Street Reform and Consumer Protection Act) that affect the structure and operations of the system.

BACKGROUND

The U.S. central banking system was established in 1913 by the Federal Reserve Act (P.L. 63-43). Congress created the Federal Reserve (popularly known as the "Fed") as an independent entity to attend to the nation's credit and monetary needs without undue influence from political pressures. Today, the Fed's monetary policy operations are intended to promote stability in the nation's economy; its supervisory and regulatory functions are intended to provide a safer, more flexible banking system; and its work as fiscal agent for the government and clearinghouse for private sector financial transactions promotes efficiency in the overall banking system.[1] In keeping with its independence within the federal government, the system operates without appropriations from Congress. Its income derives primarily from interest on government securities acquired through monetary policy operations, and fees for banking services, with any excess income returned to the Treasury.

The current structure of the system has three major components established by the original act. First, a Board of Governors oversees the whole system and has responsibility for monetary policy. Second, there are 12 regional Federal Reserve Banks, which carry out supervision and examination of commercial banks that are Fed members. The member banks, all national banks and all state-chartered banks that choose to be members of the system, make up the third component.

BOARD OF GOVERNORS

The Board of Governors of the Federal Reserve System was established as a federal government agency. The Administration and Congress can have a significant influence on the Fed through control over appointments to the seven-member board. Each of the seven governors is appointed by the President, with the advice and consent of the Senate. The full term of service for a board seat is 14 years and governors may be named to a vacant seat at any point during the term. The appointments are staggered with one term expiring every two years. Governors serving a full term may not be reappointed. Two members hold the leadership positions of chairman and vice chairman of the board.[2] They are designated by the President, with the advice and consent of the Senate. The term of service for both leadership offices is four years; an office holder may be reappointed. These terms do not coincide with that of the President or each other. Although the board chairman is considered quite powerful, each governor has one vote on the board.

When selecting a governor, the President is required by law to give due regard to a fair representation of financial, agricultural, industrial, and commercial interests, and geographical divisions of the country. No more than one governor can be selected from any one Federal Reserve district. The members of the Board of Governors cannot hold any office, position, or employment in any member bank during the time they are in office and for two years after.

At present, there are six governors; one position is vacant. The board chairman is Ben S. Bernanke, whose term as chairman ends in January 2014 and whose term as governor expires in 2020. The vice chairman is Janet L. Yellen, whose term as vice chairman expires in October 2014 and whose term as governor ends in 2024. Governor Elizabeth A. Duke is serving in a term that ends in 2012. Governor Sarah Bloom Raskin is serving in a term that ends in 2016. Governor Kevin M. Warsh is serving in a term that ends in 2018. Governor Daniel K. Tarullo is serving in a term that ends in 2022.

MONETARY POLICY

A central responsibility of the Board of Governors of the Federal Reserve System is the formulation of monetary policy. In broad terms, monetary policy involves "influencing the monetary and credit conditions in the economy in pursuit of maximum employment, stable prices, and moderate long-term interest rates."[3] In addition, when the Federal Reserve was established, it was given the role of "lender of last resort" to the nation's financial system.

The Federal Open Market Committee (FOMC) is the policy making body for open market operations—the principal means through which monetary policy is conducted. The seven board members plus five of the 12 Federal Reserve Bank presidents make up the FOMC. The president of the Federal Reserve Bank of New York (New York Fed) is a permanent member because the New York Fed executes the Federal Reserve's monetary policy decisions through open market operations. The remaining four seats are filled by the other 11 presidents on a rotating basis for one-year terms. All of the presidents participate in the FOMC meetings and contribute their views, but only the five members vote. The committee elects a chairman and vice chairman. Traditionally, the chairman of the Board of Governors is elected chairman of the FOMC and the New York Fed's president is elected vice chairman.

Open market operations involve the purchase and sale of government securities in the secondary market by the Federal Reserve. The operations are conducted to keep the federal funds rate close to a target rate that is set by the FOMC. The Federal Reserve System's portfolio is composed of U.S. Treasury securities, federal agency securities, and bankers acceptances. The Federal Reserve Bank of New York holds the portfolio and through its trading desk conducts open market operations pursuant to directives of the FOMC.

Two less often used monetary policy instruments may be employed by the Federal Reserve— legal reserve requirements and the discount window. Depository financial institutions are required by law to set aside reserves in certain proportions against demand deposits. What is held in reserve affects the availability of loanable funds. An increase in the requirement would mean banks and thrifts would have less money to lend and would tend to restrain credit conditions. Alternatively, lowering the requirement would increase the proportion of deposits that could be lent and would tend to ease credit conditions. Reserve requirements are rarely changed because as a monetary policy tool they are considered too blunt an instrument.

The discount window is the Federal Reserve facility for lending to eligible depository institutions. An institution may borrow funds for short periods from a Federal Reserve Bank to augment its reserve balances for interbank transactions. The discount rate is the interest rate charged for this short-term loan. The rate is set by each Bank subject to approval by the Board of Governors; over time, it has become common practice for the rate to be uniform for all 12 Reserve Banks. A higher rate discourages borrowing and in turn lending by banks and thrifts. Currently, the discount window serves mainly a signaling function that acts as a complement to open market operations.[4]

In response to the financial crisis that emerged in 2007, the Federal Reserve employed several new tools (in addition to the traditional ones) designed to support the liquidity of depository and other financial institutions and to foster improved conditions in financial markets.[5] The implementation of these new tools resulted in significant changes to the Federal Reserve's balance sheet. During the crisis, the Federal Reserve used its broad emergency authority under Section 13(3) of the Federal Reserve Act to authorize many actions that targeted parts of the financial system outside of the banking system. The Federal Reserve has stated it will continue to employ its policy tools as necessary to support the economic recovery.[6]

SUPERVISION AND REGULATION

The Board of Governors has a broad range of supervisory and regulatory responsibilities that affect the entire U.S. banking system.[7] The board seeks to promote safety and soundness, ensure compliance with laws and regulation, and foster the fair and efficient delivery of services to customers of financial institutions. Federal Reserve Board regulations implement policies set by Congress that are defined in legislation and referred to the Federal Reserve for enforcement. For example, the Fed has implementation and enforcement responsibilities for the Truth in Lending Act, the Electronic Funds Transfer Act, and the Fair Housing Act. The board coordinates its activities with other federal and state regulatory agencies. The board has the power to examine all member banks and their affiliates and to require periodic reports from them.

The board has the primary responsibility for supervising and regulating bank holding companies and state-chartered banks that are members of the Federal Reserve System. In addition, the board supervises corporations through which U.S. banks conduct operations abroad, and the U.S. operations of foreign banks. The board delegates many supervisory duties to the 12 Reserve Banks subject to the board's policy and oversight. An example is the task of conducting bank examinations.

The Board of Governors has broad oversight and supervisory authority over the operations and activities of the Federal Reserve Banks. The board appoints three of the nine directors of each Bank. The board conducts annual financial examinations of the Reserve Banks. Major expenditures, such as building construction, must be approved by the board. The salaries of Reserve Bank presidents and first vice presidents are subject to board approval.

FEDERAL RESERVE BANKS

The 12 Federal Reserve Banks carry out the day-to-day operations of the Federal Reserve System. Within each geographic district a city was designated as the location of the Reserve Bank. The act also provided for branch offices to support the operations of the Federal Reserve Banks. The 12 Banks are located in Boston, New York, Philadelphia, Cleveland, Richmond, Atlanta, Chicago, St. Louis, Minneapolis, Kansas City, Dallas, and San Francisco. The Board of Governors has established 25 branches over the years.

Each Federal Reserve Bank is managed by a nine-member board of directors that is divided into three classes: A, B, and C. They serve three-year terms on a staggered basis. The three Class A and Class B directors are elected by the member banks in each district. Three Class C directors are appointed by the Board of Governors. The three Class A directors represent the interests of the member banks. The remaining six directors represent the general public and are selected with due consideration to the interests of agriculture, commerce, industry, services, labor, and consumers. Class B and C directors cannot be officers, directors or employees of any banking institution. In addition, Class C directors cannot hold stock in a bank or bank holding company. The board designates one Class C director as chairman and another as deputy chairman. Each Reserve Bank is headed by a president nominated by the nine directors subject to the approval of the Board of Governors.[8]

The District Banks are the principal medium through which the general supervisory powers of the Fed are executed. Federal Reserve Banks conduct on-site examinations of state member banks and inspections of bank holding companies and their nonbank subsidiaries.

The Federal Reserve Banks provide fiscal agency and depository services to the federal government. For example, as fiscal agents they issue, transfer, exchange and redeem government securities and savings bonds. As depositories, they provide transaction accounts for the Treasury and they collect and disburse funds on behalf of the federal government.

The 12 Reserve Banks provide banking services to depository financial institutions. The Banks maintain reserve and clearing accounts for banks and thrifts. The Banks play a major role in the nation's payment system. Reserve Banks move coin and currency into and out of circulation. They also participate in the collection and processing of millions of checks daily. The Banks are an integral part of electronic funds transfer systems, clearing and settling electronically originated credits and debits.

The income of the Federal Reserve Banks is primarily generated from interest on government securities acquired through open market operations. In addition, the Monetary Control Act of 1980 requires the Federal Reserve to charge fees for various services. From their earnings the Reserve Banks pay their operating and other expenses. The Banks are assessed semiannually by the Board of Governors for the board's costs and expenditures. The residual earnings are turned over to the U.S. Treasury. Payments to the Treasury in 2009 totaled $47.4 billion.[9]

MEMBER BANKS

The Federal Reserve Act requires all national banks to be members of the Federal Reserve System. National banks are banks chartered by the federal government. Membership by state-chartered banks is optional. If state-chartered banks elect to become members they must meet standards set by the Board of Governors. As of June 30, 2009, there were 1,502 national banks and 844 state-chartered Federal Reserve member banks. While these member banks represented only about 34% of all federally insured U.S. banks, they held about 80% of all insured bank assets.[10] The 12 Reserve Banks are "owned" by their member banks. The stock of the Federal Reserve Banks is held entirely by the member banks in their respective districts. Ownership of this stock does not carry the usual rights of control and financial interest ordinarily associated with being a shareholder in a corporation operated for the purpose of making a profit. Each member bank buys stock in its district Reserve Bank equal to 6% of its own capital and surplus. Of this amount, 3% must be paid-in and 3% is subject to call by the Board of Governors. The stock may not be sold or pledged as security for loans. Dividends are set by law at the rate of 6% per year on paid-in stock.

CONGRESSIONAL OVERSIGHT

Throughout the history of the Federal Reserve System, Congress has been concerned with achieving a balance between assuring independence for the system's operations and making the agency accountable for its actions. Attention to Federal Reserve accountability has resulted in increased disclosure by the Fed and dialogue between the Fed and Congress on monetary policy and the agency's operations overall. Avenues of communication and oversight, both formal and informal, have developed over time.

Aside from its appointment role, Congress exercises oversight in a variety of ways. The Federal Banking Agency Audit Act (P.L. 95-320) was enacted in 1978 to enhance congressional oversight responsibilities. The law gave the General Accounting Office (GAO; now the Government Accountability

Office) the authority to audit the Board of Governors, the Reserve Banks and branches. Such audits are limited, however, as GAO is prohibited from auditing monetary policy operations, foreign transactions, and the FOMC operations.[11] Congressional oversight on these matters is exercised through the requirement for reports and through semi-annual monetary policy hearings, described further below.

REPORTS AND HEARINGS

The Federal Reserve publishes numerous reports during the year which are important to the oversight work of Congress. The Board of Governors publishes an annual report of activities which includes the minutes of the FOMC meetings. The board is required by law to report annually on compliance with its consumer regulations. The Federal Reserve issues reports and surveys on a variety of subjects, for example an annual survey of bank fees and services and a report on the profitability of credit card operations.

The Fed is frequently called upon to testify on a wide range of issues affecting the economy and the banking industry. In addition, a monetary policy reporting system, accomplished through hearings, was made a matter of legislative mandate in the Federal Reserve Reform Act of 1977 (P.L. 95-188). The process was modified by provisions embodied in P.L. 95-523, the Humphrey-Hawkins Act of 1978. The provisions are designed to enhance the dialogue on monetary policy between Congress and the Federal Reserve through a more detailed reporting and evaluation process than existed earlier. Further, the provisions are intended to contribute to the ability of Congress to take a coordinated look at government economic policies. The two goals are sought through a system of regularly scheduled oversight hearings at which the Federal Reserve reports to the banking committees on its policy intention. The banking committees in turn report to their respective chambers.

The statutory requirements for semi-annual monetary policy reporting, the board's annual report and several other reports would have been discontinued by provisions of the 1995 Federal Reports Elimination and Sunset Act (P.L. 104-66). Provisions contained in P.L. 106-569, enacted on December 27, 2000, reinstated these requirements.

RECENT CONGRESSIONAL ACTION

P.L. 111-203, the Dodd-Frank Wall Street Reform and Consumer Protection Act, was enacted on July 21, 2010. The omnibus financial regulatory reform law contains provisions that change the supervisory authority of the Federal Reserve Board and affect the operations and structure of Federal Reserve Board and the 12 Reserve Banks.[12]

Currently, the Federal Reserve Board has the primary responsibility for supervising and regulating bank holding companies and state-chartered banks that are members of the Federal Reserve System. Under the provisions of P.L. 111-203, the Federal Reserve will now regulate both bank and thrift (savings and loan) holding companies. The Federal Reserve will continue to regulate state-chartered banks that are members of the Federal Reserve System. In addition, the law authorizes the Federal Reserve to regulate systemically significant firms identified by the Financial Stability Oversight Council (provisions in P.L. 111-203 create this new council).

P.L. 111-203 establishes a second vice chairman position for the Board of Governors. A member of the board would be designated by the President, with the advice and consent of the Senate, to serve as vice chairman for supervision. The duties of this vice chairman would include developing policy recommendations regarding supervision and regulation for the board. The vice chairman of supervision will report to Congress semiannually on the efforts of the board with respect to the conduct of supervision and regulation.

The law contains additional oversight and disclosure provisions with the intent of increasing the transparency of Federal Reserve operations. Included is a required GAO audit of all of the 13(3) emergency lending by the Federal Reserve during the recent financial crisis and the authority for future GAO audits of 13(3) emergency lending, discount window lending, and open market transactions. Provisions delay disclosure of the identity of borrowers and the terms of loans.

P.L. 111-203 changes the procedures for choosing the Federal Reserve Bank presidents. As was described above, each Federal Reserve Bank is managed by a nine-member board of directors that is divided into three classes: A, B, and C. Class A and Class B directors are elected by the member banks in each district. The three Class C directors are appointed by the Board of Governors. The three Class A directors represent the interests of the member banks and the remaining six directors represent the general public. Currently, Reserve Bank presidents are appointed by the nine directors. Under P.L. 111-203, Class A directors will no longer vote for Reserve Bank presidents. In addition, the law requires the GAO to conduct a study of the current system for appointing directors to examine whether the system effectively represents the general public.

End Notes

[1] For an examination of the policy actions initiated by the Federal Reserve to manage and contain the current financial crisis and further financial stability, see CRS Report RL34427, *Financial Turmoil: Federal Reserve Policy Responses*, by Marc Labonte.

[2] Provisions of P.L. 111-203 add a leadership position, please see the "Recent Congressional Action" section of this report.

[3] Board of Governors of the Federal Reserve System, *The Federal Reserve System: Purposes and Functions*, p. 1, available at http://www.federalreserve.gov/pf/pdf/pf_1.pdf.

[4] For more information on monetary policy, see CRS Report RL30354, *Monetary Policy and the Federal Reserve: Current Policy and Conditions*, by Marc Labonte.

[5] For in depth information on the Federal Reserve's responses to the financial crisis, please see CRS Report RL34427, *Financial Turmoil: Federal Reserve Policy Responses*, by Marc Labonte.

[6] The Federal Reserve has a dedicated section on its website that provides information on monetary policy actions, please see
http://www.federalreserve.gov/monetarypolicy/default.htm. For information specific to the crisis response click on Credit and Liquidity Programs and the Balance Sheet.

[7] Provisions of P.L. 111-203 expand the supervisory and regulatory responsibilities of the Federal Reserve. Please see the "Recent Congressional Action" section of this report.

[8] Provisions of P.L. 111-203 make a change in the election of Federal Reserve Bank presidents. Please see the "Recent Congressional Action" section of this report.

[9] Federal Reserve Board press release, see
http://www.federalreserve.gov/newsevents/press/other/20100421b.htm.

[10] U.S. Federal Reserve System, *2009 Annual Report of the Board of Governors of the Federal Reserve System*, June 2010, p. 446.

[11] Provisions of P.L. 111-203 expand the GAO's audit authority. Please see the "Recent Congressional Action" section of this report.

[12] For an in depth discussion of the major provisions in P.L. 111-203 involving the Federal Reserve System, see CRS Report R41384, *The Dodd-Frank Wall Street Reform and Consumer Protection Act: Systemic Risk and the Federal Reserve*, by Marc Labonte and CRS Report R41339, *The Dodd-Frank Wall Street Reform and Consumer Protection Act: Titles III and VI, Regulation of Depository Institutions and Depository Institution Holding Companies*, by M. Maureen Murphy.

In: The Federal Reserve
Editor: John P. Ranchett

ISBN: 978-1-62100-528-5
© 2011 Nova Science Publishers, Inc.

Chapter 2

MONETARY POLICY AND THE FEDERAL RESERVE: CURRENT POLICY AND CONDITIONS[*]

Marc Labonte and Joseph R. McCormack

SUMMARY

The Federal Reserve (Fed) defines monetary policy as the actions it undertakes to influence the availability and cost of money and credit. Since the expectations of market participants play an important role in determining prices and growth, monetary policy can also be defined to include the directives, policies, statements, and actions of the Fed that influence how the future is perceived. In addition, the Fed acts as a "lender of last resort" to the nation's financial system, meaning that it ensures continued smooth functioning of financial intermediation by providing financial markets with adequate liquidity. This role has become of great importance following the onset of the recent financial crisis.

Traditionally, the Fed has three means for achieving its goals: open market operations involving the purchase and sale of U.S. Treasury securities, the discount rate charged to banks who borrow from the Fed, and reserve requirements that governed vault cash or deposits with the Fed as a proportion of deposits. Historically, open market operations have been the primary means for executing monetary policy. Recently, in

---

[*] This is an edited, reformatted and augmented version of a Congressional Research Service publication, CRS Report for Congress RL30354, from www.crs.gov, dated June 15, 2011.

response to the financial crisis, direct lending has become important once again and the Fed has created a number of new ways for injecting reserves, credit, and liquidity into the banking system, as well as making loans to firms that are not banks. As financial conditions normalize, the Fed is moving back to a reliance on open market operations.

The Fed traditionally conducts open market operations by setting an interest rate target that it believes will allow it to achieve price stability and maximum sustainable employment. The interest rate targeted is the federal funds rate, the price at which banks buy and sell reserves on an overnight basis. This rate is linked to other short-term rates and these, in turn, influence longer-term interest rates. Interest rates affect interest-sensitive spending such as business capital spending on plant and equipment, household spending on consumer durables, and residential investment. Through this channel, monetary policy can be used to stimulate or slow aggregate spending in the short run. In the long run, monetary policy mainly affects inflation. A low and stable rate of inflation promotes price transparency and, thereby, sounder economic decisions by households and businesses.

The Fed has frequently changed the federal funds target to match changes in expected economic conditions. Beginning June 30, 2004, the target was raised from 1% to 51/4% in 17 equal increments ending on June 29, 2006. No further changes were made until September 18, 2007, when, in a series of 10 moves, the target was reduced to a range of 0% to 1/4% on December 16, 2008, where it now remains. Since then, the Fed has added liquidity to the financial system beyond what is needed to meet its federal funds target through direct lending and, more recently, purchases of Treasury and government sponsored enterprise (GSE) securities. This practice is sometimes referred to as quantitative easing, which has tripled the size of the Fed's balance sheet since financial turmoil began. A second round of quantitative easing began in November 2010.

Congress has delegated responsibility for monetary policy to the Fed, but retains oversight responsibilities to ensure that the Fed is adhering to its statutory mandate "maximum employment, stable prices, and moderate long-term interest rates." H.R. 245 would switch to a single mandate of price stability. The Dodd-Frank Act enhanced the GAO's ability to audit the Fed, including the ability to review its lending programs. H.R. 459/H.R. 1496/S. 202 would remove all remaining restrictions on GAO's audit powers. H.R. 1512 would remove the regional Fed bank presidents from the Federal Open Market Committee.

INTRODUCTION

Congress has delegated responsibility for monetary policy to the Federal Reserve, but retains oversight responsibilities to ensure that the Fed is adhering to its statutory mandate of "maximum employment, stable prices, and moderate long-term interest rates."[1] The Federal Reserve's (Fed's) responsibilities as the nation's central bank fall into four main categories: monetary policy, ensuring financial stability through the lender of last resort function, supervision of bank holding companies, and providing payment system services to financial firms and the government. This report will discuss the first two areas of responsibility.[2]

The Fed defines monetary policy as the actions it undertakes to influence the availability and cost of money and credit to promote the goals mandated by Congress. Since the expectations of households as consumers and businesses as the purchasers of capital goods exert an important influence on the major portion of spending in the United States, and these expectations are influenced in important ways by the actions of the Fed, a broader definition of monetary policy would include the directives, policies, statements, forecasts of the economy, and other actions by the Fed, especially those made by or associated with the chairman of its Board of Governors, the nation's central banker.[3]

In addition, governments have traditionally assigned to a central bank the role of "lender of last resort" to the nation's financial system. This role means that the Federal Reserve is responsible for ensuring the sustainability, solvency, and continued functioning of the nation's financial system as a whole, although this does not necessarily extend to any individual financial institution. Thus, in times of financial stress or crisis, the Fed is responsible for ensuring that financial intermediation does not come to a halt. Historically, Federal Reserve intervention has been limited to the banking system. Indeed, the impetus for the founding of the Fed was an outgrowth of the financial panic of 1907. During its nearly 100-year history, the Federal Reserve has rarely been called upon to perform this role. It is now widely regarded as having failed to perform it during the collapse of the U.S. banking system in the contraction of 1929-1933. However, the financial crisis that began in the summer of 2007 with the bursting of the "housing price bubble" has placed this role front and center. The Fed has responded in the conventional way by making massive additions of reserves available to depository institutions (primarily commercial banks) through the purchase of U.S. Treasury securities and through lending facilities. In addition, it has created a number of additional ways to make credit available to a broader range of financial institutions as well as making loans directly to non-bank financial intermediaries. These innovations were unprecedented and several were authorized only in "unusual and exigent circumstances."[4]

Thus, the Federal Reserve has a monetary policy function and a financial stability function. Its monetary policy function is one of aggregate demand management. The availability and cost of credit are used to manage aggregate demand in such a way as to promote a stable price level and through it maximum sustainable employment. Its financial stability function is as "lender of last resort" to the nation's financial system.

The financial crisis and the Fed's unprecedented response to it has garnered renewed attention from Congress. On the one hand, the Fed was given new regulatory requirements in The Dodd-Frank Wall Street Reform and Consumer Protection Act (P.L. 111-203) in an attempt to prevent future crises. On the other hand, some Representatives have pressed for enhanced oversight of the Fed, while others have called for narrowing the scope of its statutory mandate. The Dodd-Frank Act allowed GAO to audit the Fed's monetary and lending activities for the first time, and the Federal Reserve Transparency Act of 2011 (H.R. 459/H.R. 1496/S. 202) would remove remaining restrictions on GAO's audit authority. H.R. 245 would change the Fed's statutory mandate to a single mandate of price stability.

This report provides an overview of monetary policy and issues for Congress.

HOW DOES THE FEDERAL RESERVE EXECUTE MONETARY POLICY?

The Federal Reserve has traditionally relied on three instruments to conduct monetary policy. Each works by altering the reserves available to depository institutions. These institutions are required to maintain reserves against their deposit liabilities, primarily checking, saving, and time (CDs). These reserves can be held in the form of vault cash (currency) or as a deposit at the Fed. The size of these reserves places a ceiling on the amount of deposits that financial institutions can have outstanding and deposit liabilities are related to the amount of assets these institutions can acquire. These assets are often called "credit" since they represent loans made to businesses and households, among others.

The Federal Reserve has three ways to expand or contract money and credit. The primary method is called open market operations and it involves the Fed buying existing U.S. Treasury securities (or those that have been already issued and sold to private investors). Should it buy securities, it does so with the equivalent of newly issued currency (Federal Reserve notes). This expands the reserve base and the ability of depository institutions to make loans and expand money and credit. The reverse is true if the Fed decides to sell securities from its portfolio.

The Fed can also change reserve requirements, controlling a portion of deposits that banks must hold as vault cash or in deposit at the Fed, which affects the available liquidity within the market.

Currently, banks with $58.8 million or more in liabilities are required to hold 10.3% of their liabilities in reserves. This tool is used rarely—the percentage was last changed in 1998.[5] To increase control over reserve growth, the Federal Reserve began to pay interest on required and excess reserves in October 2008, reducing the opportunity cost of holding that money as opposed to lending it out.

Finally, the Fed permits certain depository institutions to borrow from it directly on a temporary basis. That is, these institutions can "discount" at the Fed some of their own assets to provide a temporary means for obtaining reserves. Discounts are usually on an overnight basis. For this privilege they are charged an interest rate called, appropriately, the discount rate. The discount rate is set by the Fed at a markup over the federal funds rate.[6] Direct lending, from the discount window and other recently created lending facilities, was negligible until late 2007, but has been an important source of reserves since then.

Because the Fed defines monetary policy as the actions it undertakes to influence the availability and cost of money and credit, this suggests two ways to measure the stance of monetary policy. One is to look at the cost of money and credit as measured by the rate of interest relative to inflation (or inflation projections), while the other is to look at the growth of money and credit itself. Thus, one can look at either interest rates or the growth in the supply of money and credit in coming to a conclusion about the current stance of monetary policy, that is, whether it is expansionary, contractionary, or neutral.

Since the great inflation of the 1970s, most central banks have preferred to formulate monetary policy more in terms of the cost of money and credit rather than on their supply. The Federal Reserve thus conducts monetary policy by focusing on the cost of money and credit as proxied by an interest rate. In particular, it targets a very short-term interest rate known as the federal funds rate. The Federal Open Market Committee (FOMC) meets every six weeks to choose a federal funds target and sometimes meets on an ad hoc basis if it wishes to change the target between regularly scheduled meetings. The FOMC is comprised of the 7 Fed governors, the President of the New York Fed, and 4 of the other 11 regional Fed bank presidents selected on a rotating basis.[7]

The federal funds rate is determined in the private market for overnight reserves of depository institutions. At the end of a given period, usually a day, depository institutions must calculate how many dollars of reserves they want to hold against their reservable liabilities (deposits).[8] Some institutions may discover a reserve shortage (too few reservable assets relative to those it wants to hold) while others may have had reservable assets in excess of their wants. A market exists in which these reserves can be bought and sold on an overnight basis. The interest rate in this market is called the federal funds rate. It is this rate that the Fed uses as a target for conducting monetary policy. If it wishes to expand money and credit, it will lower the target which encourages more lending activity and, thus, demand in the economy. To support this lower target, the Fed must stand ready to buy more U.S. Treasury securities. Conversely, if it wishes to tighten money and credit, it will raise the target and remove as many reserves from depository institutions as are necessary to accomplish its ends. This will require the sale of treasuries from its portfolio of assets.[9]

The federal funds rate is linked to the interest rates that banks and other financial institutions charge for loans—or the provision of credit. Thus, while the Fed may directly influence only a very short-term interest rate, this rate influences other longer-term rates. However, this relationship is far from being on a one-to-one basis since the longer-term market rates are influenced not only by what the Fed is doing today, but what it is expected to do in the future and what inflation is expected to be in the future. This highlights the importance of expectations in explaining market interest rates. For that reason, there is a growing body of literature that urges the Federal Reserve to be very transparent in explaining what its policy is and will be and making a commitment to adhere to that policy. In fact, the Fed has responded to this literature and is increasingly transparent in explaining its policy measures and what these are expected to accomplish.

Using market interest rates as an indicator of monetary policy is fraught with danger, however. The interest rate that is essential to decisions made by households and businesses to buy capital goods is what economists call the "real" interest rate. It is often proxied by subtracting from the market interest rate the actual or expected rate of inflation. The real rate is largely independent of the amount of money and credit since over the longer run, it is determined by the interaction of saving and investment (or the demand for capital goods). The internationalization of capital markets means that for most developed countries the relevant saving and investment that determines the real interest rate is on a global basis. Thus, real rates in the United States depend not only on our national saving and investment, but on the saving and investment of other countries as well. For that reason national interest rates are influenced by international credit conditions and business cycles.

The recent financial crisis underlines that open market operations alone can be insufficient at times for meeting the Fed's statutory mandate. Since the crisis, many economists and central bankers have argued that a macroprudential approach to supervision and regulation is needed, and this may affect conduct of monetary policy to maintain maximum employment and price stability.[10] Whereas traditional open market operations managed to contain systemic risk following the bursting of the "dot-com" bubble in 2000, direct lending by the Fed on a large scale was unable to contain systemic risk in 2008. In a recent speech, Fed Chairman Bernanke said he is committed to serving on and working closely with the Financial Stability Oversight Committee, created by the Dodd-Frank Act, to safeguard against systemic risk.[11] He also described how the Fed has recently restructured its internal operations to facilitate a macroprudential approach to supervision and regulation.[12]

Economic Effects of Monetary Policy in the Short Run and Long Run

How do changes in short-term interest rates affect the overall economy? In the short run, an expansionary monetary policy that reduces interest rates increases interest-sensitive spending, all else equal. Interest-sensitive spending includes physical investment (i.e., plant and equipment) by firms, residential investment (housing construction), and consumer-durable spending (e.g., automobiles and appliances) by households. As discussed in the next section, it also encourages exchange rate depreciation that causes exports to rise and imports to fall, all else equal. To reduce spending in the economy, the Fed raises interest rates, and the process works in reverse. An examination of U.S. economic history will show that money- and credit-induced demand expansions can have a positive effect on U.S. GDP growth and total employment. The extent to which greater interest-sensitive spending results in an increase in overall spending in the economy in the short run will depend in part on how close the economy is to full employment. When the economy is near full employment, the increase in spending is likely to be dissipated through higher inflation more quickly. When the economy is far below full employment, inflationary pressures are more likely to be muted. This same history, however, also suggests that over the longer run, a more rapid rate of growth of money and credit is largely dissipated in a more rapid rate of inflation with little, if any, lasting effect on real GDP and employment. (Since the crisis, the historical relationship between money growth and inflation has not held so far, as will be discussed below.)

Economists have two explanations for this paradoxical behavior. First, they note that, in the short run, many economies have an elaborate system of contracts (both implicit and explicit) that makes it difficult in a short period for significant adjustments to take place in wages and prices in response to a more rapid growth of money and credit. Second, they note that expectations for one reason or another are slow to adjust to the longer run consequences of major changes in monetary policy. This slow adjustment also adds rigidities to wages and prices. Because of these rigidities, changes in the growth of money and credit that change aggregate demand can have a large initial effect on output and employment albeit with a policy lag of six to eight quarters before the broader economy fully responds to monetary policy measures. Over the longer run, as contracts are renegotiated and expectations adjust, wages and prices rise in response to the change in demand and much of the change in output and employment is undone. Thus, monetary policy can matter in the short run but be fairly neutral for GDP growth and employment in the longer run.[13]

It is noteworthy that in societies where high rates of inflation are endemic, price adjustments are very rapid. During the final stages of very rapid inflations, called hyperinflation, the ability of more rapid rates of growth of money and credit to alter GDP growth and employment is virtually nonexistent, if not negative.

Monetary vs. Fiscal Policy

Either fiscal policy (defined here as changes in the structural budget deficit) or monetary policy can be used to alter overall spending in the economy. However, there are several important differences to consider between the two.

First, economic conditions change rapidly, and in practice monetary policy can be much more nimble than fiscal policy. The Fed meets every six weeks to consider changes in interest rates, and can call an unscheduled meeting any time in between. Large changes to fiscal policy typically occur once a year at most. For example, there were three large tax cuts from the 2001 recession through 2006;[14] in the same period, interest rates were changed 29 times. Once a decision to alter fiscal policy has been made, the proposal must travel through a long and arduous legislative process that can last months before it can become law, while monetary policy changes are made instantly.[15]

In addition to differences in implementation lags, both monetary and fiscal policy face lags due to "pipeline effects." In the case of monetary policy, interest rates throughout the economy may change rapidly, but it takes longer for economic actors to change their spending patterns in response. For example, in response to a lower interest rate, a business must put together a loan proposal, apply for a loan, receive approval for the loan, and then put the funds to use. In the case of fiscal policy, once legislation has been enacted, it may take some time for authorized spending to be outlayed. An agency must approve projects and select and negotiate with contractors before funds can be released. In the case of transfers or tax cuts, recipients must receive the funds and then alter their private spending patterns before the economy-wide effects are felt. For both monetary and fiscal policy, further rounds of private and public decision-making must occur before "multiplier" or "ripple" effects are fully felt.

Second, political constraints has led to fiscal policy being employed mostly in only one direction. Over the course of the business cycle, aggregate spending in the economy can be expected to be too high as often as it is too low. This means that stabilization policy should be tightened as often as it is loosened, yet increasing the budget deficit has proven to be much more popular than implementing the spending cuts or tax increases necessary to reduce it. As a result, the budget has been in deficit in all but five years since 1961. This has led to an accumulation of federal debt that gives policymakers less leeway to potentially undertake a robust expansionary fiscal policy, if needed, in the future. By contrast, the Fed is more insulated from political pressures,[16] and experience shows that it is as willing to raise interest rates as it is to lower them.

Third, the long run consequences of fiscal and monetary policy differ. Expansionary fiscal policy creates federal debt that must be serviced by future generations. Some of this debt will be "owed to ourselves," but some (presently, about half) will be owed to foreigners. To the extent that expansionary fiscal policy "crowds out" private investment, it leaves future national income lower than it otherwise would have been.[17] Monetary policy does not have this effect on generational equity though different levels of interest rates will affect borrowers and lenders differently. Furthermore, the government faces a budget constraint that limits the scope of expansionary fiscal policy—it can only issue debt as long as investors believe that the debt will be honored—even if economic conditions require larger deficits to restore equilibrium.[18]

Fourth, openness of an economy to highly mobile capital flows changes the relative effectiveness of fiscal and monetary policy. Expansionary fiscal policy would be expected to lead to higher interest rates, all else equal, which would attract foreign capital looking for a higher rate of return.[19] Foreign capital can only enter the United States on net through a trade deficit. Thus, higher foreign capital inflows lead to higher imports, which reduces spending on domestically produced substitutes, and lower spending on exports. The increase in the trade deficit would cancel out the expansionary effects of the increase in the budget deficit to some extent (in theory, entirely). This theory is supported by experience—as the budget deficit increased, so did the trade deficit.[20] Expansionary monetary policy would have the opposite effect—lower interest rates would cause capital to flow abroad in search of higher rates of return elsewhere. Foreign capital outflows would reduce the trade deficit through an increase in spending on exports and domestically produced import substitutes. Thus, foreign capital flows would (tend to) magnify the expansionary effects of monetary policy.

Fifth, fiscal policy can be targeted to specific recipients. In the case of normal open market operations, monetary policy cannot. This difference could be considered an advantage or disadvantage. On the one hand, policymakers could target stimulus to aid the sectors of the economy most in need, or most likely to respond positively to stimulus. On the other hand, stimulus could turn out to be allocated on the basis of political or non-economic factors that reduce the macroeconomic effectiveness of the stimulus. As a result, both fiscal and monetary policy have distributional implications, but the latter's are largely incidental, whereas the former's can be explicitly chosen.

In cases where economic activity is extremely depressed, monetary policy may lose some of its effectiveness. When interest rates become extremely low, interest-sensitive spending may no longer be very responsive to further rate cuts. Furthermore, interest rates cannot be lowered below zero. In this scenario, fiscal policy may be more effective. As is discussed in the next section, some would argue that the U.S. economy experienced this scenario following the recent financial crisis.

Of course, using monetary and fiscal policy to stabilize the economy are not mutually exclusive policy options. But because of the Fed's independence from Congress and the Administration, the two policy options are not always coordinated. If compatible fiscal and monetary policies are chosen by Congress and the Fed, respectively, then the economic effects would be more powerful than if either policy were implemented in isolation. For example, if stimulative monetary and fiscal policies were implemented, the resulting economic stimulus would be larger than if one policy were stimulative and the other were neutral. But if incompatible policies are selected, they could partially negate each other. For example, a stimulative fiscal policy and contractionary monetary policy may end up having little net effect on aggregate demand (though there may be considerable distributional effects). Thus, when fiscal and monetary policymakers disagree in the current system, they can potentially choose policies with the intent of offsetting each others' actions.[21] Whether this arrangement is better or worse for the economy depends on what policies are chosen. If one actor chooses inappropriate policies, then the lack of coordination usefully allows the other actor to try to negate its effects.

THE RECENT AND CURRENT STANCE OF MONETARY POLICY

Until financial turmoil emerged in 2007, a consensus had emerged among economists that a relatively stable business cycle could be maintained through prudent and nimble changes to interest rates via transparently communicated and signaled open market operations. That consensus would break down as the financial crisis worsened, as the Fed took increasingly unconventional and unprecedented steps to restore financial stability.

Before the Financial Crisis

As the U.S. economy was coming out of the short and shallow 2001 recession, unemployment continued rising until mid-2003. Fearful that the economy would slip back into recession, the Fed kept the federal funds rate extremely low.[22] The federal funds target reached a low of 1% by mid-2003. As the expansion gathered momentum and prices began to rise, the federal funds target was slowly increased in a series of moves to 5 1/4% in mid-2006.

It is now argued by some economists that the financial crisis was, at least in part, due to Federal Reserve policy to ensure that the then-ongoing expansion continued.[23] In particular, critics now claim that the low short-term rates were kept too low for too long after the 2001 recession had ended, and this caused an increased demand for housing that resulted in a "price bubble." The shift in financing housing from fixed to variable rate mortgages made this sector of the economy increasingly vulnerable to movements in short-term interest rates. An alternative perspective, championed by Chairman Bernanke and others, was that the low mortgage rates that helped fuel the housing bubble were mainly caused by a "global savings glut" over which the Fed had little control.[24] One consequence of the tightening of monetary policy later in the decade, critics now claim, was to burst this "price bubble" (a bubble that was also due, in part, to lax lending standards that were subject to regulation by the Fed and others).

During and after the Financial Crisis

The bursting of the housing bubble led to the onset of a financial crisis that affected both depository institutions and other segments of the financial sector involved with housing finance. As the delinquency rates on home mortgages rose to record numbers, financial firms exposed to the mortgage market suffered capital losses and lost access to liquidity. The contagious nature of this development was soon obvious as other types of loans and credit became adversely affected. This, in turn, spilled over into the broader economy, as the lack of credit soon had a negative effect on both production and aggregate demand. In December 2007, the economy entered a recession.

As the spillover effects from the housing slump to the financial system, as well as its international scope, became apparent, the Fed responded by reducing the federal funds target and the discount rate.[25] Beginning on September 18, 2007, and ending on December 16, 2008, the target was reduced from 5 1/4% to a range between 0% and 1/4%, where it currently remains.

With liquidity problems persisting as the federal funds rate was reduced, it appeared that the traditional transmission mechanism linking monetary policy to activity in the broader economy was not working. It also, began to concern the monetary authorities that the liquidity provided to the banking system was not reaching other parts of the financial system. Under traditional monetary policy tools, additional monetary stimulus cannot be provided once the federal funds rate has reached its zero bound. To circumvent this problem, the Fed decided to use more nontraditional methods to provide additional monetary policy stimulus.

First, the Federal Reserve introduced a number of emergency credit facilities to provide increased liquidity directly to financial firms and markets. The first facility was introduced in December 2007, and several were added after the worsening of the crisis in September 2008. These facilities were designed to fill perceived gaps between open market operations and the discount window. The loans primarily provided by these facilities were designed to provide short-term loans backed by collateral that exceeds the value of the loan.[26] A number of the recipients were non-banks that are outside the regulatory umbrella of the Federal Reserve; this marked the first time that the Fed lent to non-banks since the Great Depression. The Fed began to employ a seldom used emergency provision, Section 13(3) of the Federal Reserve Act,[27] that allows it to make loans to other financial institutions and to non-financial firms as well. The Fed justified their pursuit of this policy on the grounds that it falls under its mandate to "promote effectively the goals of maximum employment, stable prices, and moderate long term interest rates."[28]

The Fed provided assistance through liquidity facilities, which included both the traditional discount window and the newly created emergency facilities previously mentioned, and through direct support to two specific institutions, AIG and Bear Stearns. The magnitude of this assistance has been large. Total assistance from the Federal Reserve at the beginning of August 2007 was approximately $234 million provided through liquidity facilities, with no direct support given. In mid-December 2008, it reached a high of $1.6 trillion, with a near high of $108 billion given in direct support. From that point on, it fell steadily. Assistance provided through liquidity facilities fell below $100 billion in February 2010, and support to specific institutions fell below $100 billion in January 2011.[29] The majority of these facilities expired at the beginning of February 2010, and all those that have expired to date saw all transactions repaid with interest.

With direct lending falling as financial conditions began to normalize and the federal funds rate at its zero bound, the Fed found other tools to maintain the elevated level of liquidity in the financial system in order to prevent a removal of monetary stimulus while the economy was still fragile. In March 2009, the Fed announced plans to purchase $300 billion of Treasury securities,

$200 billion of Agency (Fannie Mae and Freddie Mac) debt (later revised to $175 billion), and $1.25 trillion of Agency mortgage-backed securities. These purchases were completed by the end of March 2010.

Beginning in November of 2010 the Federal Reserve, dissatisfied with the high level of unemployment, took steps to encourage economic growth by purchasing an additional $600 billion of Treasury securities and continuing the practice of replacing maturing securities. The purchases were made at a pace of $75 billion a month and were completed in about six months. The Fed has focused on purchasing securities with maturities between 2 1/2 and 10 years in length.[30] According to the Fed, these actions were taken to promote a stronger pace of economic recovery because current progress towards the Fed's policy objectives has been "disappointingly slow."[31]

This is clearly not a "business as usual" monetary policy, but something quite extraordinary, sometimes referred to as "quantitative easing." While there may not be a universally accepted definition of quantitative easing, this report defines it as actions to further stimulate the economy through growth in the Fed's balance sheet once the federal funds rate has reached the "zero bound."

The Growth in the Balance Sheet and Bank Reserves

The assistance provided by the Federal Reserve to banks and non-bank institutions is considered an asset on the Federal Reserve balance sheet because it represents money owed to or assets owned by the Fed. This assistance and its holdings of Treasury securities, mortgage-backed securities and government sponsored enterprise debt comprise most of the assets on the Fed's balance sheet.

From the time its first emergency lending facility was introduced in December 2007 until the crisis worsened in September 2008, the Fed "sterilized" the effects of lending on its balance sheet by selling Treasury securities. After September 2008, the Fed allowed its balance sheet to grow, and between September and November 2008, it more than doubled in size, increasing from under $1 trillion to over $2 trillion. The increase in assets during this time took the form of direct assistance through emergency facilities.

From November 2008 to November 2010, the overall size of the Fed's balance sheet did not vary much; however, its composition changed. As of December 2010, loans made up $46 billion of the $2,427 billion of the Fed's balance sheet and securities made up $2,225 billion. When the purchases of

Treasury securities announced in November 2010 is complete, the balance sheet is expected to be about $600 billion larger.

This increase in the Fed's assets must be matched by a corresponding increase in its liabilities on its balance sheet, mostly in the form of currency, bank reserves, and cash deposited by the U.S. Treasury at the Fed. Bank reserves increased from about $46 billion in August 2008 to $820 billion at the end of 2008 to $1,138 billion at the end of 2009. As of January 2011 total reserves still remained high with $1,077 billion still being held by banks. The increase in bank reserves can be seen as the inevitable outcome of the increase in assets held by the Fed because they, in effect, financed the Fed's asset purchases and loan programs. The lending facilities increased reserves because the loan amounts are credited to the recipients' reserve accounts at the Fed.[32]

Whether the additional reserves will be lent out by banks, resulting in lower market interest rates and an expansion of new spending, as posited in the textbook explanation of how monetary policy works, is another story. Recent experience is not reassuring, as the large volume of reserves added to the banking system by the Fed have remained as excess bank reserves. Some economists fear that the response of banks to additional reserves is a sign that the economy has entered a "liquidity trap," where total spending in the economy (aggregate demand) is unresponsive to additional monetary stimulus. This phenomenon could help explain why the unprecedented growth in the monetary base (the portion of the money supply controlled by the Fed) has not translated into higher inflation to date. Critics fear that it is simply a matter of time before quantitative easing leads to high inflation, and argue that these long-term risks outweigh any modest short-term benefits.[33]

By contrast, the Fed has argued that quantitative easing has successfully stimulated the economy, mainly through lower long-term interest rates.[34] Janet Yellen, Vice Chair of the Board of Governors of the Federal Reserve System, defended these policies in a recent speech. She argues that the evidence has shown that the financial securities purchases by the Federal Reserve have proven effective in easing financial conditions. With unemployment remaining high and expectations that inflation will be low over the medium run, she argues that the accommodative stance of the Fed regarding their monetary policy is appropriate.[35]

CONGRESSIONAL OVERSIGHT AND DISCLOSURE

Humphrey-Hawkins Hearings

Congress has delegated monetary policy decisions to the Fed but retains oversight responsibilities. A primary form of congressional oversight of the Federal Reserve is the semiannual hearings with the Senate Committee on Banking, Housing, and Urban Affairs and the House Committee on Financial Services. At these hearings, which take place in February and July, the Fed Chairman presents the Fed's *Monetary Policy Report to the Congress*, testifies, and responds to questions from committee members. These hearings and reporting requirements were established by the Full Employment Act of 1978 (P.L. 95-523, 92 Stat 1897), also known as the Humphrey-Hawkins Act, and renewed in the American Homeownership and Economic Opportunity Act of 2000 (P.L. 106-569).

The semiannual *Monetary Policy Report* presents a review of recent economic and monetary policy developments, as well as economic projections for three years. Since monetary policy plays an important role in determining economic outcomes, these projections can be viewed as the Fed's perceptions of how today's monetary policy stance will influence future economic conditions. To increase the transparency of monetary policy, the Fed in 2007 began to publicly provide additional forecasts. They now appear quarterly.

GAO Audits

In the wake of the financial crisis there was a strong push to remove the statutory restrictions on the Government Accountability Office's (GAO's) ability to audit the Fed. This restriction was modified by Title XI of the Dodd-Frank Wall Street Reform and Consumer Protection Act (P.L. 111-203).[36] As a result, the GAO can now audit the Fed's monetary actions and lending programs for issues such as operational integrity, accounting and financial reporting, and internal controls, but is still unable to conduct policy evaluations of those activities. Further, any confidential information that the GAO gathers cannot be released until it is first made public by the Fed.

Some Representatives have pressed for greater GAO oversight than provided in the Dodd-Frank Act. The Federal Reserve Transparency Act of 2011 (H.R. 459/H.R. 1496/S. 202) would remove remaining audit restrictions and require a GAO audit of the Fed.

Disclosure of Lending Records

As a result of another section of the Dodd-Frank Act, the Fed is required, for the first time, to publicly disclose information on the identities of borrowers, amount borrowed, rate charged, and collateral pledged or assets transferred within one year after a credit facility is terminated and within two years after the transaction for discount window loans or open market operations. On December 1, 2010, the Federal Reserve released the summary of all transactions made since December 1, 2007, under programs created during the crisis; however, this release did not include information on discount window transactions. Separately, Bloomberg and Fox News Network sued the Federal Reserve under the Freedom of Information Act for the release of internal records pertaining to lending activities, including the discount window, for the period of August 2007 to March 2010. As a result, the Fed released this information on March 31, 2011.

Greater disclosure and outside evaluation could potentially help Congress perform its oversight duties more effectively. A main argument against increasing Fed oversight would be that it could be perceived to reduce the Fed's operational independence from Congress. While few policymakers argue for total independence or total disclosure and oversight, the policy challenge is to strike the right balance between the two. The Fed's independence is discussed in the next section.

THE FEDERAL RESERVE'S MANDATE AND ITS INDEPENDENCE

The Constitution grants Congress the power to "coin money, and regulate the value thereof.... " However, operational responsibility for making U.S. monetary policy has been delegated by Congress to the Fed. Congress is still responsible for oversight, setting the Fed's mandate and approving the President's nominations for the Fed's Board of Governors, but several institutional features grant it significant "independence" from the political process.[37] The Federal Reserve system is quasi-public in structure: its regional banks are owned by its member banks. The governors are appointed to staggered 14-year terms, and can only be removed by Congress for cause. It is self-funded and its budget is not subject to the congressional appropriation process. It has been granted broad *discretion* to interpret and carry out its congressional mandate as it sees fit on a day-to-day basis.

Although the Fed's statutory mandate might be expected to be a significant curb on its independence, The Federal Reserve Act of 1977 (P.L. 95-188, 91 Stat. 1387) charged the Fed with "the goals of maximum employment, stable prices, and moderate long-term interest rates." Note that the Fed controls none of these three indicators directly; it controls only overnight interest rates through the use of open market operations, the discount window, and reserve requirements. There will be times when the goals will be at odds with each other, and the Fed will have to choose to pursue one at the expense of the other two. For example, an energy price shock would be expected to raise prices and reduce employment. In this case, the current mandate could be used to justify expansionary monetary policy in response to lower employment or contractionary monetary policy in response to higher prices. Critics have argued that the ambiguity inherent in the current mandate makes for less than optimal transparency and accountability. It may also strengthen political independence if it allows the Fed to deflect congressional criticism by pointing, at any given time, to whatever goal justifies its current policy stance.

The most popular alternative to the current mandate is to replace it with a single mandate of price stability.[38] H.R. 245 is an example of such a bill in the 112th Congress. This proposal is often coupled with a proposal for the Fed to be given (or, under the version mooted by Chairman Bernanke, give itself) a numerical inflation target, and the Fed would then be required to set monetary policy with the goal of meeting the target on an ongoing basis. Proponents of inflation targeting say that maximum employment and moderate interest rates are not meaningful policy goals because monetary policy has no long-term influence over either one. They argue a mandate that is focused on keeping inflation low would deliver better economic results and improve transparency and oversight.[39] Opponents, including former Fed chairman Greenspan, say that the flexibility inherent in the current system has served the United States well in the past 25 years, delivering both low inflation and economic stability, and there is little reason to fix a system that is not broken. They argue that some focus on employment is appropriate given that monetary policy has powerful short-term effects on it, and that too great a focus on inflation could lead to an overly volatile business cycle. Various forms of inflation targeting have been adopted abroad.[40] Other economists argue that a single mandate would do little to curb the Fed's independence, and would therefore have little practical effect on its decision making.

Most economists argue that central bank independence leads to good monetary policy because it reduces the temptation to raise inflation in the long run in order to lower unemployment in the short run. Researchers have made cross-country comparisons to try to make the case that countries with independent central banks are more likely to have low inflation rates and better economic performance.[41] As noted in the previous section, independence from Congress may make oversight less effective, however.

End Notes

[1] Section 2A of the Federal Reserve Act, 12 USC 225a.
[2] For background on the make up of the Federal Reserve, see CRS Report RS20826, *Structure and Functions of the Federal Reserve System*, by Marc Labonte.
[3] For a discussion of the important role played by expectations in formulation and execution of monetary policy, see Santomero, Anthony M. "Great Expectations: The Role of Beliefs in Economics and Monetary Policy." *Business Review,* Federal Reserve Bank of Philadelphia. Second Quarter 2004, pp. 1-6, and Sellon, Gordon H., Jr., "Expectations and the Monetary Policy Transmission Mechanism," *Economic Review,* Federal Reserve Bank of Kansas City, Fourth Quarter 2004, pp. 4-42.
[4] For a discussion of the 2007-2009 financial crisis, its origins, and the innovations by the Federal Reserve, see CRS Report RL34427, *Financial Turmoil: Federal Reserve Policy Responses*, by Marc Labonte. For historical perspective on Federal Reserve's dealing in non-government debt, see Wheelock, David C. "Conducting Monetary Policy Without Government Debt: The Fed's Early Years. *Review,* Federal Reserve Bank of St. Louis. May/June 2002, pp. 1-14.
[5] The deposit threshold is regularly adjusted for inflation. The Dodd-Frank Act encouraged regulators to implement heightened liquidity standards, particularly for Systemically Important Financial Institutions (SIFIs), that may affect reserve requirements once fully implemented. The status of SIFI regulation was discussed in a speech by Federal Reserve Governor Daniel Tarullo on June 3, 2011. The speech can be seen at http://www.Federal reserve.gov/ newsevents/speech/tarullo20110603a.htm.
[6] Until 2003, the discount rate was set slightly below the federal funds target, and the Fed used moral suasion to discourage healthy banks from profiting from this low rate. To reduce the need for moral suasion, lending rules were altered in early 2003. Since that time, the discount rate has been set at a penalty rate above the federal funds rate target. However, during the financial crisis, the Fed encouraged banks to use the discount window.
[7] H.R. 1512 would remove the regional Fed bank presidents from the Federal Open Market Committee.
[8] Depository institutions are obligated by law to hold some fraction of their deposit liabilities as reserves. In addition, they are also likely to hold additional or excess reserves based on certain risk assessments they make about their portfolios and liabilities. Until very recently these reserves were non-income earning assets. The Fed now pays interest on both types of reserves. It is too early to assess how this shift in policy will affect bank reserve holdings.

[9] For a technical discussion of how this is actually done, see Edwards, Cheryl L., "Open Market Operations in the 1990s," *Federal Reserve Bulletin*, November 1997, pp. 859-872.

[10] Bank for International Settlements, "Monetary Policy in a World with Macro Prudential Policy," speech by Jaime Caruana on June 11, 2011, http://www.bis.org/speeches/sp110610.htm.

[11] For more information, see CRS Report R41384, *The Dodd-Frank Wall Street Reform and Consumer Protection Act: Systemic Risk and the Federal Reserve*, by Marc Labonte.

[12] Chairman Ben Bernanke, "Implementing a Macroprudential Approach to Supervision and Regulation," speech at the 47th Annual Conference on Bank Structure and Competition, Chicago, Illinois, Federal Reserve, May 5, 2011, http://www.federalreserve.gov/newsevents/speech/bernanke20110505a.htm.

[13] Two interesting papers bearing on what monetary policy can accomplish by two former officials of the Federal Reserve are Santomero, Anthony M. "What Monetary Policy Can and Cannot Do," *Business Review*, Federal Reserve Bank of Philadelphia, First Quarter 2002, pp. 1-4, and Mishkin, Frederic S. "What Should Central Banks Do?," *Review*, Federal Reserve Bank of St. Louis, November/December 2000, pp. 1-14.

[14] The tax cuts are the Economic Growth and Tax Relief Reconciliation Act (P.L. 107-16), the Job Creation and Worker Assistance Act (P.L. 107-147), and the Jobs and Growth Tax Relief Reconciliation Act (P.L. 108-27).

[15] To some extent, fiscal policy automatically mitigates changes in the business cycle without any policy changes because tax revenue falls relative to GDP and certain mandatory spending (such as unemployment insurance) rises when economic growth slows, and vice versa.

[16] For more information, see CRS Report RL31056, *Economics of Federal Reserve Independence*, by Marc Labonte.

[17] An exception to the rule would be a situation where the economy is far enough below full employment that virtually no crowding out takes place because the stimulus to spending generates enough resources to finance new capital spending.

[18] The analogous constraint on monetary policy is that after a certain limit, expansionary monetary policy would become highly inflationary. But from the current starting point of price stability, problems with inflation would presumably only occur after a point where the economy had returned to full employment.

[19] For more information, see CRS Report RL31235, *The Economics of the Federal Budget Deficit*, by Brian W. Cashell.

[20] See CRS Report RS21409, *The Budget Deficit and the Trade Deficit: What Is Their Relationship?*, by Marc Labonte and Gail E. Makinen.

[21] It is important to take this possibility into consideration when evaluating the potential effects of fiscal policy on the business cycle. Because the Fed presumably chooses (and continually updates) a monetary policy that aims to keep the economy at full employment, the Fed would need to alter its policy to offset the effects of any stimulative fiscal policy changes that moved the economy above full employment. Thus, the actual net stimulative effect of a fiscal policy change (after taking into account monetary policy adjustments) could be less than the effects in isolation.

[22] Historical and current targets for the federal funds rate can be found at http://www.federalreserve.gov/fomc/ fundsrate.htm.

[23] In a WSJ opinion article, six economists are polled regarding if the Fed was to blame for creating the housing bubble that in part led to the recent financial crisis, and five of six responded that the Fed in some degree was to blame. See David Henderson, "Did the Fed Cause the Housing Bubble?," *Wall Street Journal*, March 27, 2009.

[24] See Ben Bernanke, "The Global Saving Glut and the U.S. Current Account Deficit," speech at the Virginia Association of Economists, March 10, 2005.
[25] For a detailed account of the Fed's role in the financial crisis, see CRS Report RL34427, *Financial Turmoil: Federal Reserve Policy Responses*, by Marc Labonte.
[26] See CRS Report R41073, *Government Interventions in Response to Financial Turmoil*, by Baird Webel and Marc Labonte.
[27] 12 U.S.C. 343.
[28] Federal Reserve Act, Section 2A, 12 USC 225a.
[29] Data from "Recent Balance Sheet Trends," *Credit and Liquidity Programs and the Balance Sheet*, http://www.federalreserve.gov/monetarypolicy/bst_recenttrends.htm. Values include totals from credit extended through Federal Reserve liquidity facilities and support for specific institutions.
[30] CRS Report R41540, *Quantitative Easing and the Growth in the Federal Reserve's Balance Sheet*, by Marc Labonte.
[31] Federal Open Market Committee, Federal Reserve, "press release," November 3, 2010, http://www.federalreserve.gov/newsevents/press/monetary/20101103a.htm.
[32] See H.3. Federal Reserve Statistical Releases, Aggregate Reserves of Depository Institutions and the Monetary Base at http://www.federalreserve.gov/releases/h3/Current.
[33] See, for example, "An Open Letter to Chairman Bernanke," November 15, 2010, http://economics21.org/ commentary/e21s-open-letter-ben-bernanke.
[34] For a recent discussion of this issue by the president of the Federal Reserve Bank of St. Louis, see Bullard, Thomas. *Effective Monetary Policy in a Low Interest Rate Environment*, The Henry Thornton Lecture, Cass Business School, London, March 24, 2009.
[35] Board of Governors of the Federal Reserve System, "2011 International Conference," speech by Janet L. Yellen on June 1, 2011, http://www.federalreserve.gov/newsevents /speech/ yellen 20110601a.htm.
[36] More details on the changes made in the Dodd-Frank Act can be found in CRS Report R40877, *Financial Regulatory Reform: Systemic Risk and the Federal Reserve*, by Marc Labonte.
[37] For more information, see CRS Report RL31056, *Economics of Federal Reserve Independence*, by Marc Labonte.
[38] See CRS Report R41656, *Changing the Federal Reserve's Mandate: An Economic Analysis*, by Marc Labonte.
[39] In a 2009 speech, then Fed Vice Chairman Donald Kohn reports that the Fed Governors and Reserve Bank presidents continue "to discuss whether an explicit numerical objective for inflation would be beneficial. Under current circumstances, those benefits would include underscoring our understanding that our legislative mandate for promoting price stability encompasses both preventing inflation from falling too low in the near term and from rising too far as the economy recovers." See *Monetary Policy in the Financial Crisis*, a Conference in Honor of Dewey Daane, Nashville, Tennessee, April 18, 2009.
[40] See CRS Report RL31702, *Price Stability (Inflation Targeting) as the Sole Goal of Monetary Policy: The International Experience*, by Marc Labonte and Gail E. Makinen.
[41] For a review of the research and criticisms, see CRS Report RL31955, *Central Bank Independence and Economic Performance: What Does the Evidence Show?*, by Marc Labonte and Gail E. Makinen.

In: The Federal Reserve
Editor: John P. Ranchett

ISBN: 978-1-62100-528-5
© 2011 Nova Science Publishers, Inc.

Chapter 3

ECONOMICS OF FEDERAL RESERVE INDEPENDENCE[*]

Marc Labonte

SUMMARY

The Federal Reserve System (Fed) is charged with responsibility for making U.S. monetary policy. Quasi-public in structure, overseen by a Board of Governors whose members are appointed to serve long terms, and reliant on its own source of funding, the Fed possesses a degree of independence that some argue is inimical to the spirit of democracy. Although this argument (and refutations of it) may be political or constitutional in nature, it is also rooted in certain notions about macroeconomic policy.

The power that the Fed wields is substantial. Along with fiscal policy, monetary policy is one of two kinds of policy that can be employed to influence aggregate demand. In the short run, both monetary and fiscal policy have the power to raise or lower employment. But they have opposite short-run effects on interest rates (expansionary monetary policy lowers interest rates and expansionary fiscal policy raises them), so that in concert they can achieve results that neither can in isolation. The long-run effects of the two policies are quite different from their short-run effects. Fiscal policy helps determine interest rates in the long run, but not the rate of inflation. Monetary policy largely determines the

---

[*] This is an edited, reformatted and augmented version of a Congressional Research Service publication, CRS Report for Congress RL31056, from www.crs.gov, dated April 17, 2007.

inflation rate, but cannot be used to fix interest rates in the long run. Policies based on the assumption that monetary policy can fix interest rates ultimately generate accelerating inflation or deflation.

Monetary policy affects inflation only after it affects employment. A policy structure that responds quickly to the immediate concerns of the public is thus more likely to generate inflation than one that allows policymakers to more easily weather bad times. A very responsive policy structure not only increases the likelihood of high inflation. It also tends to produce more business cycles if policy directed at reducing inflation is aborted before it is complete, only to be reintroduced again later when the renewed expansion makes inflation worse. On-again, off-again policies erode the credibility of the monetary authorities and make anti-inflation policy all the more costly and lengthy when it is undertaken in earnest.

Reducing the independence of the Fed either means reducing the ability to engage in discretionary policy or shifting economic power to the executive branch. This is an important consideration given the difficulty in calibrating policy. Because the legislative branch is not in a position to exercise day-to-day control of monetary policy, if it wishes to reduce the Fed's discretionary powers, it must choose between establishing policy rules to which the Fed must adhere or allowing the executive to administer policy. Economists who oppose rules fear that they would be too rigid to deliver economic stability in a highly complex economy.

Better coordination of monetary and fiscal policy is a double-edged sword. If "good" policy is pursued, it will be all that much better if simultaneously pursued with both tools. But if "bad" policy is pursued, using both tools to pursue it will make the result that much worse. Thus, the choice boils down to whether the policy structure should be one that maximizes the benefits that come from policy when it is well chosen or minimizing the costs that occur when policy is ill-advised.

INTRODUCTION

The Constitution grants Congress the power to "coin money, and regulate the value thereof...." Congress has delegated responsibility for making U.S. monetary policy to the Federal Reserve System (Fed). This latter arrangement is one that many observers have criticized. Quasi-public in structure, overseen by a Board of Governors whose members are appointed to long terms, and reliant on its own source of funding, the Fed possesses a degree of independence that some argue is inimical to the spirit of democracy.

Although this argument (and refutations of it) may be political or constitutional in nature, it is also rooted in certain notions about macroeconomic policy. Debates concerning the ability of the Fed to control interest rates, the need for coordination of monetary policy and fiscal policy, or even the importance of monetary policy, underlie the arguments for and against independence, and are matters of economic analysis.

Thus, in undertaking a discussion of whether the Fed should have more or less independence or accountability, it is essential to understand how monetary policy works, and its role relative to fiscal policy. Without this knowledge, it is possible that a decision to change the structure of the Fed would fail to bring about the economic effects desired, or would bring about other, adverse, effects not expected by advocates of the change.

This report[1] gives a brief description of the structure of the Fed. It then discusses the economics of how Fed independence affects monetary policy. The report does not consider how Fed independence may affect the Fed's other duties, such as its oversight of the financial system. It then examines the probable economic ramifications of proposals to curb the independence of the Fed.

STRUCTURE OF THE FEDERAL RESERVE SYSTEM

Background

While there are many economic arguments supporting Fed independence, it is interesting to note that none of these arguments—nor the primary duties of today's Fed that underlie these arguments—existed when the Fed was founded. Yet its structure today was largely determined in its earliest years.

The Federal Reserve System was created largely in response to the panic of 1907 and the many banking panics of the late 19th century. This is ironic, since the Fed later presided over the country's worst series of banking panics in 1930-1933; federal deposit insurance would have to be created to prevent a reoccurrence of banking panics. Moreover, part of the Fed's original mandate, to create an "elastic currency," is believed to be an expression of the "real bills doctrine," a notion held in low regard within the economics profession today. As one author states, it is "high on the list of longest lived economic fallacies of all time."[2] Its job now, to conduct monetary policy, was not believed by most experts at the time of its creation to be a proper or even possible function of government. Before the 1930s, macroeconomic stabilization policy was not widely developed, and when it emerged from the Great Depression, monetary policy was seen as having little independent power to influence the economy and was just the helpmate of the more powerful fiscal policy. The Fed's principal method of undertaking monetary policy, open market operations, was not even envisioned at its creation; the technique of influencing the money supply through the sale and purchase of securities on the open market was inadvertently discovered during the early years of its existence as the Fed attempted to manage its portfolio of assets. For these reasons, it is not all that surprising that some observers believe that the Fed's structure is not well suited to its job.

Current Structure

The Fed's structure has been changed several times since it was established. Its current structure, however, is largely the same as that which emerged in the late 1930s. U.S. monetary policy is determined within the Federal Reserve System. At the top of the system is the seven-member Board of Governors appointed to staggered 14-year terms by the President with Senate advice and consent. No member may be reappointed to a new term after having served a full term. By the same appointment and approval process, a Chairman and Vice Chairman are selected from the seven to serve four-year terms. These terms do not coincide with that of the President. The President can remove Fed governors "for cause" before their term has ended, but not on the basis of policy differences or incompatibility.[3] In practice, the President has never done so. The Chairman of the Fed, though considered quite powerful, has only one vote on the Board. His power derives principally from setting the Board's agenda, from his role as the Fed's representative in meetings with other government officials, and from his control of the Board's staff.

There are 12 regional Federal Reserve Banks, which were established in the belief that the system should safeguard against a concentration of power in New York or Washington. Each is set up as a private operation owned by member banks, with a nine-member Board of Directors. Six of the Board members are selected by member banks and three by the Board of Governors, including a chairman and deputy chairman. The Board of Directors then appoints the president and first vice president of its regional bank, subject to Board of Governors approval.[4]

The seven members of the Board of Governors sit with the president of the New York Federal Reserve Bank and four other regional bank presidents, who are selected on a rotating basis among the other 11 regional banks, on the

Federal Open Market Committee (FOMC). The FOMC is responsible for determining the target for the federal funds rate, which is the inter-bank overnight lending rate. The target is maintained through open market operations, which is the principal tool of monetary policy. The discount rate, which is the rate at which the Fed lends to liquidity-constrained banks, is set by the Board alone upon application by a regional bank for a change.

Money is placed into circulation through the purchase of U.S. Treasury securities. Because the system holds a large portfolio of securities, it earns income. Essentially, this is income from money creation and it is technically referred to as seigniorage. Member banks are the shareholders of the Federal Reserve Banks, and a dividend is paid to member banks corresponding to their stake in the system. After operating costs are deducted, and additions are made to its capital account (to maintain solvency), the rest is remitted to the Treasury, where it is recorded as "miscellaneous receipts." In 2005, it was estimated that 92% of the Fed's profits, or $21.5 billion, was remitted to the U.S. Treasury. About 3% of its profits were paid in dividends to shareholder banks and 5% were added to its capital.

The way in which the Fed earns and passes on income means, first, that the government receives the revenue from money creation just as it would if, say, the Treasury administered monetary policy instead of the Fed. It means, second, that the Fed does not need a congressional appropriation of funds to operate. It has its own source of revenue and can conduct policy free of concern that budgetary pressure might be applied by those wanting to influence its decisions.

Although the Fed has great latitude in implementing monetary policy, the goals that it is mandated to achieve through monetary policy are determined by Congress. In this sense, monetary policy is neither independent nor undemocratic. Having said that, both opponents of the Fed's independence and many economists would agree that the Fed's current mandate is broad and vague, and, therefore, greatly enhances its independence for better or for worse. Its charge derives from the legislation that created it (Federal Reserve Act, P.L. 63-43), from which comes its responsibility to provide an "elastic currency"; the Federal Reserve Reform Act of 1977 (P.L. 95-188), which directs it to maintain stable prices, maximum employment, moderate interest rates, and sustainable growth; and the Full Employment and Balanced Growth Act of 1978 (P.L. 95-523), which requires it to relate its policy to the employment goals of the entire federal government set pursuant to the aims of the Employment Act of 1946 (P.L. 79-304).

As will be shown below, these goals frequently conflict. Collectively, they amount to telling the Fed that it is to make good economic policy. Given that these goals often cannot all be pursued simultaneously, and that some—even by themselves—can only be sustained temporarily, the Fed can usually find legislative authority for any monetary stance it assumes.

THE GOALS OF MONETARY POLICY

Many recessions occur because aggregate supply exceeds aggregate demand. In other words, total spending is lower than what the economy is capable of producing. Economists attribute this phenomenon to the presence of price stickiness. When the demand for goods and labor falls, prices should fall to a point where adequate demand is restored. But because price adjustment does not happen quickly—due to the presence of contracts, menus, and uncertainty—output declines. This can lead to a vicious cycle where unemployment rises and resources fall idle— lowering aggregate demand further. In the long run, prices will adjust and the economy will return to its full potential. However, the examples of the Great Depression and the Japanese economy in the 1990s suggest that the long run can be very long indeed.

If the government does not wish to wait for this long run self-adjustment to occur, it has two primary tools at its disposal to boost aggregate demand. The favored tool at present is monetary policy. The Fed can inject newly printed money into the economy by purchasing U.S. Treasuries, a process referred to as expansionary monetary policy. Since prices do not adjust instantly, this money will increase aggregate output if there are unused resources in the economy. The channel through which this spending increase occurs is lower interest rates. The cost of borrowing is lowered as the reserves available to the banking system expand. Thus, aggregate spending is boosted through higher investment spending on capital goods, equipment, and buildings and through higher consumption on interest-sensitive goods like automobiles, homes, and appliances. Aggregate spending is also boosted through the foreign trade sector. Lower interest rates attract less investment to the United States, and, other things being equal, this reduces demand for the dollar. As the exchange rate depreciates, foreign spending on U.S. exports and the U.S. production of import-competing goods will rise.[5]

In the long run, the printing of money can have no real effect on the economy—sustained inflation is a purely monetary phenomenon. Reductions in unemployment resulting from expansionary monetary policy are either temporary (if the economy was already at full employment when policy was changed) or would have eventually occurred anyway (if the economy was not at full employment). Prices will adjust to the increase in the money supply, causing inflation to rise. The closer the economy is to its full potential when monetary policy becomes expansionary, the more the increase in aggregate demand will be transmitted into higher inflation rather than greater output.

Differences between Fiscal and Monetary Policy

Another stabilization tool at the government's disposal is fiscal policy. The government can boost its spending and finance it through an increase in its budget deficit (or a reduction in its surplus). This increases aggregate demand directly by increasing the government's purchase of goods and services. Similarly, the government can cut taxes through a smaller surplus or larger deficit, which boosts household spending by increasing disposable income (assuming that households spend the tax cut rather than save it). But unlike expansionary monetary policy, expansionary fiscal policy results in rising, rather than falling, interest rates, other things being equal. Interest rates rise because deficits are financed out of private saving. That results in the availability of less private saving for private capital investment. The demand for investment on a smaller pool of saving bids up the price of that saving, the interest rate. When the economy is deep in recession, the demand for investment may be very weak, and deficit spending will cause little upward pressure on interest rates. By contrast, if the economy is operating near full potential when expansionary fiscal policy is undertaken, then interest rates will rise substantially, crowding out most of the increase in aggregate demand caused by expansionary fiscal policy.[6]

When interest rates rise, foreign investment is attracted to the country, offsetting some of the decline in saving available for investment. However, this causes the dollar exchange rate to appreciate, which reduces foreign demand for U.S. exports and U.S. demand for import-competing goods. This also crowds out the boost in demand caused by expansionary fiscal policy to the extent that it causes interest rates to rise. Thus, as the U.S. has become more open to international capital flows and trade, monetary policy has become more powerful and fiscal policy less powerful. That is because exchange rate effects work to reinforce the effects of monetary policy on aggregate demand but offset the effects of fiscal policy.

Unlike monetary policy, expansionary fiscal policy cannot lead to a sustained increase in the inflation rate—there is some limit beyond which the deficit will stop rising, even if it remains high. First of all, the deficit cannot exceed 100% of aggregate spending. Even before that point, the deficit must stop growing if the public can no longer reasonably believe that government bonds they purchase will be honored. But the money supply can keep growing as long as it is allowed to do so. As long as some people are willing to hold money, the money supply can grow; many historical examples of hyperinflation suggest that some people will hold money even at extremely high monetary growth rates.

While the ability of fiscal policy to raise or lower inflation is only temporary, monetary policy can only raise or lower (inflation-adjusted) *interest rates* temporarily. Using monetary expansion to push rates down in an economy that is fully employed will just stimulate higher prices. These higher prices will offset the initial depressing effect that expansionary monetary policy had on interest rates since the Fed has not changed the resources available in the economy for investment. On the other hand, fiscal policy can have a permanent effect on interest rates. A high level of government borrowing, even if the level is constant, can hold interest rates up indefinitely because of its effects on the saving available for investment.

Thus, in the short run both fiscal and monetary policy increase economic growth and inflation. But expansionary fiscal policy results in higher interest rates, whereas expansionary monetary policy results in lower interest rates. Likewise, contractionary fiscal policy lowers growth and inflation with lower interest rates as a result, whereas contractionary monetary policy leads to higher interest rates. In the long run, monetary and fiscal policy have very different influences, however. Fiscal policy helps determine the interest rate, monetary policy does not. Monetary policy determines the inflation rate, fiscal policy does not. Neither can permanently boost the long-run economic growth rate; this is determined by the growth rate of labor, capital, and productivity.

Policy Calibration, Lags, and the Role of Credibility

Obviously, not all the adjustments referred to above occur immediately. Otherwise there would be no short run imbalances and the economy would always be at full employment. Experience teaches that this is not the case. Historical evidence indicates that the full price effects from fiscal and monetary policy come roughly two years after the policy is implemented.

Employment effects come much faster, within two or three quarters. The reason for this asymmetry in lags is price stickiness. Although hard to quantify, expectations play an important role here as well. If individuals expect inflation to accelerate or decelerate, it will do so more quickly, even if policymakers claim to desire otherwise.

The closer the economy is to full employment when demand management is undertaken, the faster the price effects will occur. But even in a fully employed economy, prices will not adjust quickly enough that output effects are zero and the full rise in inflation is immediate. Growth will be boosted, but the boom will be unsustainable and short lived. The legacy of expansionary policy will be higher inflation. Similarly, if faced with undesirably high inflation, contractionary policy will reduce output and increase unemployment in the short run. Only later will prices adjust to slow inflation.

Moreover, how long it takes inflation to slow down in response to contractionary policy, and how long higher unemployment must be endured, depend on the credibility of the central bank's anti-inflation plan. If the public thinks that a contractionary policy will soon be abandoned, then prices will not be adjusted, and inflation and heightened unemployment will be slow to abate.

The role of credibility, expectations, and the state of the economy all result in variability in the length of the policy lag and the magnitude of the output response. Thus, it is difficult to design a policy with any precision that can systematically counteract the various pressures, which themselves are often poorly understood, that tend to generate swings in economic activity. This means not only is it impossible to calibrate policy well enough to avoid business cycles, but that attempts to do so may even make the cycles worse. In hindsight, some economists have blamed many recessions on monetary policy errors.

CRITICISMS OF INDEPENDENCE

Criticisms of the Fed's structure break down to three notions. First, some believe the Fed is too independent in the sense that its decisions are too far removed from the will of the public. Second, critics say that monetary and fiscal policy are made in isolation from each other, so that there is no mechanism to guarantee their coordination. Third, others argue that as an institution, the Fed is insufficiently open or accountable, with its activities shrouded in secrecy and with little external supervision or examination of its outlays, management practice, and policy decisions.

In general, both those who argue for continued broad discretion and those who argue for change emphasize the importance of monetary policy for the economy and make it the center of their arguments. Basically, one side maintains that monetary policy is too important to be put into the hands of a few appointed officials. The other believes that it is too important not to do so.

While monetary policy is important, one must keep in mind how it is important. The short-run effects of monetary policy differ substantially from its long-run effects. Whatever argument is advanced to support or attack independence, it should not be predicated on the belief that the Fed's job is to control interest rates. The Fed's influence over the economy is short-term only. In the long run the Fed does not control real interest rates, and efforts aimed at controlling interest rates based on its short-run influence generally result in accelerating inflation or deflation.

Independence

Whereas fiscal policy is made jointly by the legislative and executive branches, monetary policy is influenced only indirectly by either. The long terms of Fed governors, the fact that they are appointed rather than elected, and the fact that the institution has its own source of funding means that Fed governors and other FOMC members are likely to be less responsive to swings in public opinion than are the makers of fiscal policy.

This does not automatically mean that the structure of the Fed is inconsistent with the traditional character of American government. For example, members of the federal judicial branch are appointed, in their case for life, and there is a constitutional prohibition on diminishing their salary while in office. It should again be stressed that the overarching goals of monetary policy are determined by Congress; it is merely the day-to-day implementation of those goals that has been delegated to an independent Fed. What makes monetary policy unusual is the fact that it is not implemented by the executive branch, whose chief is directly elected but is otherwise staffed by civil servants and appointees serving at the discretion of the chief. Thus, at issue is not whether the Fed's independence is unique in our government—it is not—but whether its independence is appropriate or advantageous for the conduct of monetary policy.

Several elements of the earlier analysis bear on this issue. First, there is the difference in the short-run and long-run effects of monetary policy. The positive employment effects from an overexpansion of the money supply are temporary and experienced in the short run. The higher rate of inflation comes later—it would not even begin to be felt for a year or two, the length of a congressional term. The economic costs of high and variable inflation are well chronicled.[7] Similarly, anti-inflation policy takes a long time to achieve its results; in the interim it causes an increase in unemployment. If elected officials seek short-term "gain" at the cost of long-term "pain," this lag structure would impart an inherent bias toward inflation. It would also tend to produce more business cycles if policy directed at reducing inflation is aborted before it is complete, only to be reintroduced again later when the renewed expansion makes inflation worse.

By insulating decision-makers from the immediate effects of public pressure, proponents point out that independence may help offset that bias. The Fed may be better able than other institutions to resist the temptation to "gun" the economy in preparation for an election. Similarly, when attempting to reduce entrenched inflation, the Fed may more easily "tough out" criticism of a contractionary policy until inflation abates, thereby avoiding a premature policy reversal that renders the already-incurred unemployment costs pointless.

This argument in favor of independence is necessarily not one for total insulation of decision making. In fact, total insulation probably does not exist: many Fed critics believe there are many historical examples that suggest that political pressure led to incorrect decisions by the Fed. What it might suggest is putting monetary policy on a "slow fuse," where outside judgement operates over a longer time horizon. Even then, the economic advantage of independence would have to be weighed against a number of non-economic factors favoring less independence.

Some proposals for change stop short of eliminating Fed independence. Whether it is worthwhile to decrease the Fed's independence by placing officials from the executive branch on the Board of Governors, or by subjecting the Fed's budget to congressional approval, is a matter of judgement of both a democratic and economic nature. But the economics of monetary policy is such that the cost of making the Fed more responsive to short-term public opinion would likely be an increased tendency to inflate the economy and to reverse anti-inflation policies before they have time to achieve their intended purpose. International evidence backs up this theory, at least when independence is broadly defined, since many central banks that do not enjoy a level of independence similar to the Fed have allowed higher inflation on average.[8]

The second element of independence, credibility, reinforces the first economic argument. In the short run, the responsiveness of inflation to changes in monetary policy depends in part on people's expectations of the Fed's behavior. Imagine that the Fed were to tighten monetary policy to reduce an uncomfortably high inflation rate. If people believed that the Fed would be unwilling to follow through with an anti-inflationary stance once unemployment rose, then people would reduce their inflationary expectations very slowly and cautiously. This would feed through into wage contracts and pricing decisions by firms that would cause inflation to be temporarily higher than expected given the change in monetary policy. Since it is sluggish price adjustment that causes unemployment to rise and output to contract in the short run, this suggests that the rise in unemployment caused by the contractionary policy would be greater and more persistent than if the central bank had greater credibility. Thus, even when a less independent central bank is resolved to pursue an anti-inflationary policy to its end, its lack of independence may lower its credibility, making the policy more painful and persistent in the short run than it otherwise would be.

Third, the alternative to an independent central bank has implications for the checks and balances of our government. Legislative bodies are not designed to administer policy; Congress could not fulfill the Fed's current task of setting discretionary policy on a day-to-day basis. Thus, Congress would have two choices: eliminate discretion through the adoption of a rule, an option considered below, or delegate the day-to-day administration of discretionary monetary policy to the administrative branch. The latter would tilt economic power significantly toward the executive. The checks and balances applicable to fiscal policy would not apply to monetary policy. Thus, eliminating the Fed's independence would not simply make the federal government more democratic; it would also have implications for the checks and balances of power that some might see as making the government less democratic.

To judge how important the economic benefits of Fed independence may be, it is useful to consider the example of fiscal policy. Like monetary policy, expansionary fiscal policy has short-run benefits, in terms of higher output and employment, and long-term costs, in terms of higher inflation and debt burdens. Perhaps the overwhelming reason why fiscal policy has fallen into disrepute with many economists as a stabilization tool is precisely because of the unwillingness of elected lawmakers to tighten fiscal policy (reduce a budget deficit) when aggregate demand is "overheating."[9] A rule of thumb for effective fiscal policy is that the budget should be balanced over the business cycle—budget deficits in recession years should be offset by surpluses in boom years. In practice, the federal budget was in deficit in 36 of 37 years between 1961and 1997, and returned to deficit in 2002 after four years of surplus.

Coordination

Some observers consider coordination an important element of Fed reform because under the current system monetary and fiscal policy are made separately. While coordination may take place, the Fed is free to follow a policy totally at odds with the fiscal stance taken by Congress and the President. It is entirely possible for monetary policy to be undoing what fiscal policy is doing with output and employment, or for monetary policy to be reinforcing the effect that fiscal policy is having on interest rates. Directed in concert, the two policies should be able to produce much more effective policy than if they are determined in isolation of each other.

In particular, using fiscal and monetary policy in concert allows aggregate demand to be influenced with minimal disruption to interest rates and the exchange rate, since fiscal policy pushes interest rates and the exchange rate in the opposite direction of monetary policy. This has several advantages. For example, if resources cannot be reallocated completely fluidly and costlessly, it may minimize the difference in output effects on particular sectors or regions of the economy in the short run. It may also prevent economic imbalances from forming or mitigate existing imbalances in the short run. Furthermore, it may make long-term business planning more predictable, since such planning is highly dependent on interest rates and exchange rates.

However, if fiscal and monetary policy were coordinated, they could also produce much worse policy. Just as a well-conceived fiscal policy can be enhanced by monetary policy designed to support it, an ill-conceived fiscal policy can become all that more damaging to the economy if reinforced by a monetary policy made to go with it. Hence, good policy can be much better if monetary and fiscal policy are coordinated, but bad policy can be made much worse.

The potential for ill-conceived coordination is particularly great due to the relative roles of the two policies in affecting interest rates and inflation. Large fiscal deficits frequently arise from a deadlock concerning whether to raise taxes or reduce spending. These deficits tend to hold interest rates higher than they would be otherwise. In systems amenable to coordination, the temptation thereby arises to use expansionary monetary policy to lower interest rates that have been forced up by fiscal policy. Since interest rates are not something that monetary policy can influence in the long run, the result is accelerating inflation, an outcome that large deficits could not achieve on their own.

In this regard, it is worth noting that studies of hyperinflations have consistently identified two essential components of the policies that ultimately brought such episodes to an end; one of them is an independent central bank capable of refusing a government's requests for money.[10] Clearly, coordination has not always proven a recipe for sound demand management policy.

The fiscal situation of the government in the 1980s and early 1990s illustrates the dilemma well. Large budget deficits tended to keep interest rates high, and relatively little progress was made in bringing deficits down until the late 1990s. Had the Fed been under the control or influence of the Administration or Congress, they would have had the option of "coordinating" this fiscal policy with more expansionary monetary policy as a solution to the problem of high interest rate effects. Since such policy is short-run in its effect, the effort to coordinate policy in this way would be inflationary.

This observation does not imply that coordination is undesirable. Rather, it highlights the cost of coordination: the risk of putting all policy eggs in one basket. The current division of economic policy responsibilities, therefore, produces yet another check-and-balance arrangement. Because of this split in responsibilities, no stabilization policy is likely to be carried very far in one direction unless consensus is achieved among different policymaking bodies.

Proposals to better coordinate monetary and fiscal policy, including placing monetary policy under the control of the Treasury, putting a Treasury official on the Board of Governors, and matching the term of the Fed chairman with that of the President, raise this balance-of-power dilemma. Opting for more or less coordination therefore boils down to a trade-off between maximizing the benefits that come from policy when it is well-chosen and minimizing the costs that occur when policy is ill-advised.

Accountability and Disclosure

The third area of concern to critics of the Fed's independence is the secrecy with which operations at the Fed are conducted. Transcripts of the FOMC's deliberations are not released for five years, and minutes of FOMC meetings are released only after the following FOMC meeting. The Board is audited by outside auditors. (Board staff audit the regional Fed banks.) The Government Accountability Office (GAO), already the auditor of a variety of sensitive government agencies and regulatory bodies, is limited in what kinds of audits it can conduct of the Fed. It is specifically prohibited from auditing the Fed's monetary policy activities.

The issue of accountability should be viewed as distinct from the issue of democracy. Democracy—in this case, the potential shifting of the powers of the Fed to elected officials—is one approach to increasing accountability, but it is not the only one. The next section considers an alternative method of increasing accountability, the use of rules. Hence, some may advocate greater Fed accountability without favoring diminished Fed independence.

There is little that economic analysis can contribute to this area of debate. Policy may be better or worse under greater public scrutiny, and whether it is or not must be judged in terms of what best makes for "good government." Accountability could have two economic effects worth exploring. First, what costs does secrecy impose on markets? Second, how would greater disclosure affect the Fed's behavior and Congress's oversight abilities?

Fed-watching engages real resources, albeit small in comparison to the overall economy, in the task of second-guessing monetary policy. In addition, costs may be imposed by market fluctuations caused by unfounded speculation over Fed policy. The rational expectations literature stresses the importance of information about both the present and the future in making efficient decisions. If the Fed's secrecy creates needless uncertainty, economic efficiency and welfare could be reduced. Presumably, if more information on Fed deliberations were available to the public these costs could be reduced.

The need to out-guess the Fed, however, does not so much result from Fed secrecy as much as from the use of discretion in monetary policymaking. The advantage in any market is in predicting events before someone else does; this is true whether market agents are trying to figure out what Fed policy is or what it will be. And as long as discretion is employed, there are limits on just how much policy can be spelled out in advance. Thus, proposals to increase disclosure (e.g., through immediate release of FOMC minutes or official statements concerning the Fed's intermediate targets) might not do much to diminish Fed-watching. Nor would a reduction in independence diminish Fed-watching if the new policy regime were based on discretion.

However, more complete disclosure might have a different benefit. It might produce better policy. The fact that the Fed can make pronouncements about policy in vague, qualitative terms allows the potential for policy to be made in an ad hoc or idiosyncratic way. Whether it does so in fact is not clear—indeed, it is impossible to judge objectively given that its pronouncements are vague. The members of the FOMC may have very definite models of economic behavior in mind when deciding whether to tighten or loosen policy. Whatever those models are, however, they are not always clear to outside observers.

Proponents of more complete disclosure believe it could promote more closely reasoned decisions about policy that reflect just what economic events are considered by the FOMC to be indicative of a certain policy, why that policy follows logically from those events, and what future events would be accepted as evidence that the policy is no longer appropriate. This view holds that fuller disclosure would force the Fed to specify its picture of the economy and thereby help ensure that one actually exists.

Better accounting of the Fed's actions could also help Congress in its oversight of Fed performance. Congress has the Congressional Budget Office (CBO) and the Joint Committee on Taxation to help provide independent evaluation of fiscal and tax policy. But it must depend on the Fed itself in assessing monetary policy much more than it does on the Treasury or Office of Management and Budget (OMB) in tax and budgetary matters. Independent evaluation of the Fed's actions on a periodic basis could put Congress in a position more analogous to that it is in when studying fiscal and tax policy.[11]

Other economists would argue that there is a limit to achieving adequate disclosure and oversight as long as the Fed explains its decisions qualitatively rather than quantitatively. For example, when reading the Fed's policy statements, some Fed watchers claim that the Fed's view of the potency of monetary policy—and hence personal culpability—sharply declines whenever there is an economic downturn. Ultimately, they argue, only rules that link hard data to policy decisions can be judged objectively.

What if Rules Replaced Discretion?

Critics of Fed independence cannot complain that the goals of monetary policy have been determined in an undemocratic fashion: the goals of the Federal Reserve are mandated by Congress. To a great extent, if the Fed's policymaking is vague and unaccountable, it is because Congress has given it a vague and oftentimes internally inconsistent mandate. Rather, opposition to Fed independence lies with the fact that unelected officials have considerable discretion in pursuing that mandate, and the fact that voters and elected representatives have limited institutional oversight to ensure that the Fed fulfills its mandate.

Since the economics of independence suggest considerable economic disadvantages would arise from shifting discretion to elected officials, most economists concerned with the status quo have focused instead on devising ways to remove discretion from monetary policy. Their efforts have focused on strengthening the Fed's mandate such that it ceases to be a fuzzy guideline and instead becomes a strict rule. With a precise enough rule, decision-making by the Fed would be largely unnecessary, and accountability would be straightforward. "Fed watching" would be unnecessary as markets would never need to second-guess what motivated policy decisions and what decisions would follow a change in economic conditions. Policy would change predictably and automatically as economic data became available.

The drawback to a rule-based policy regime lies in the fact that the Fed does not precisely or directly control the variables with which it is most concerned—notably, inflation or the growth rate of aggregate demand. Its interest rate decisions influence these variables, but imprecisely, variably, and with long lags in their effectiveness. Thus, rules based on the variables of ultimate concern cannot be applied in a straightforward and easily verifiable fashion. Alternatively, the variables that the Fed can control are not variables that influence society's economic welfare in and of themselves. A rule could direct the Fed to cause the money supply to grow at a certain rate, to fix short term interest rates at a certain level, to fix the exchange rate value of the dollar, or to keep the price of gold constant. But none of these rules would be directly related to economic stability. Targeting the growth rate of the money supply or the price of gold would not deliver economic stability because neither are predictably or systematically related to economic growth or inflation. Fixing interest rates would not provide economic stability because the Fed only controls the supply of short-term credit. Variability in the demand for credit means that different interest rates are appropriate at different times. Fixing the exchange rate may increase external stability, but is unrelated to internal stability. The other drawback to a rule is that since the Fed has only one tool, it can potentially target only one variable with any precision. But it is concerned with at least two variables, inflation and the growth of aggregate demand. More goals dilute the effect that its policy tool has on each particular goal.

This difference between policy goals and the policy tools available explains why discretion exists in the first place. If there were a simple relationship between the Fed's actions and their effect on inflation and unemployment, the Fed would not need to use its discretion in determining the proper policy. The minority of economists who see the Fed itself as the primary cause of economic instability in the 20th century would argue that any strict rule, regardless of how directly related to inflation and demand growth, would lead to greater economic stability than discretionary policy. But most economists accept that economic stability rests upon the use of monetary policy to stabilize inflation and demand growth. Those who accept this but oppose discretion have endorsed the "Taylor rule," developed by economist John Taylor, now Undersecretary of the Treasury. Under a Taylor rule, the Fed would automatically alter interest rates based on a simple equation that responds to changes in inflation and output growth. Detractors of this and other rules stress that interest rate changes do not always influence the economy predictably, uniformly, or promptly; thus, the use of a rule could potentially be destabilizing, particularly in times of crisis.[12]

Between the polar alternatives of complete discretion and strict rules lies a spectrum of looser rules that would reduce but not eliminate the Fed's discretion. The most famous of these is an inflation target, which has been adopted by several foreign central banks, including the European Central Bank and the Bank of England.[13] An inflation target would mandate that the sole goal of monetary policy is to keep the inflation rate equal to a predetermined rate (or within a predetermined band) in the long run. But unlike a strict rule, central bankers would remain free to use their discretion to reach their target. If this rule were strictly interpreted, it would be quite strict indeed—even small increases in inflation would lead to sharp increases in interest rates under any circumstances, and vice versa. But it could be destabilizing since demand growth would be neglected entirely. For instance, an oil shock could simultaneously cause a recession and an acceleration in the inflation rate. A strict inflation target would require the central bank to raise interest rates, worsening the recession. In practice, foreign central banks have proven quite responsive to changes in demand growth, even when inflation is above its target. And their mandate has typically included many caveats and exemptions to ensure flexibility. This raises the criticism that inflation targets have not meaningfully reduced discretion—central bankers are still free to do as they see fit.

Viewed objectively, an inflation target strikes a balance between rules and discretion, and enjoys some of the benefits but suffers from some of the drawbacks of both. Under an inflation target, it seems unlikely that inflation would be allowed to get out of hand for long without ramifications.[14] Central bankers could no longer justify any policy stance by pointing to conflicting parts of their mandate. In this way, accountability would be increased. On the other hand, an inflation target as practiced still lacks a quantifiable way to evaluate specific discretionary decisions. As economists Ben Bernanke and Frederic Mishkin (now Chairman and Governor of the Federal Reserve, respectively) argue, "constrained discretion" is probably a more apt description of the international experience with inflation targets.[15]

Would a rule-based monetary policy be a more democratic arrangement than discretionary control by unelected officials? The answer to that question is beyond the scope of this report. Economist Milton Friedman, for one, believed it would be more democratic. In Friedman's eyes, the contrast between rules and discretion in monetary policy was analogous to the contrast between the Bill of Rights and leaving decisions of individual liberty in the hands of the legislature. He reasoned satirically,

> Why not take up each (free speech) case separately and treat it on its own merits? Is this not the counterpart to the usual argument in monetary policy that it is undesirable to tie the hands of the monetary authority in advance; that it should be left free to treat each case on its merits as it comes up? Why is not the argument equally valid for speech?[16]

CONCLUSION

An argument against independence cannot be predicated on the belief that interest rates can be fixed or that inflation and recession could always be avoided if interest rates were never raised. Instead, an economically valid argument against independence can be made as long as it recognizes that the positive effects interest rate reductions have on output and employment come sooner than the negative effects interest rate reductions have on inflation. Similarly, anti-inflation policies bring short-term pain and only long-term rewards.

In such circumstances, independence, or partially insulating the Fed from short-term political pressures through institutional arrangements, is a way to make painful but necessary policies more likely to occur. There are also some possible economic drawbacks to independence that merit consideration. First, oversight is difficult in the current system, and this makes it difficult to prevent or reverse poor policy decisions by the Fed. Second, potential benefits of coordinating monetary and fiscal policy cannot be secured. While disallowing coordination means that the benefits of good policy cannot be maximized, it also means that the effects of bad policy can potentially be minimized.

If reducing or eliminating Fed independence were deemed too economically costly, are there alternative reforms that could be considered to address the issues that critics have raised? Monetary policy rules are another way to make policy immune from detrimental short term pressures, and they do not suffer from some of the drawbacks of independence. Rules would also boost accountability and some might view them as more democratic in the sense that they reduce the discretionary power of unelected officials. The economic tradeoff between rules and discretion is of a different nature. It boils down to a question of how well a highly complex economy can be stabilized by a blunt and simple rule. Economists are highly divided on this point. Many of those who support rules do so because they have little faith in the ability of the FOMC to make better discretionary decisions than a simple rule.

An inflation target, as it has been practiced abroad, is a modest middle path between strict policy rules and unlimited discretion, but only because it has not been implemented too literally. Congressional oversight suffers from having the Fed's goals as vaguely defined as they are at present. An inflation target would tighten those goals and increase accountability if persistently egregious policy errors were made. It would not, however, significantly reduce the Fed's independence as it attempted to devise discretionary monetary policy for a highly complex and changing economy.

The economic arguments for and against Fed independence evaluated in this report apply only to the Fed's monetary policy responsibilities. Arguments for and against reassigning the Fed's other duties, such as bank regulation, to a less independent entity are beyond the scope of this report.

End Notes

[1] This report revises and expands upon an earlier CRS report written by G. Thomas Woodward. His previous contribution is gratefully acknowledged.

[2] Mark Blaug, *Economic Theory in Retrospect*, Cambridge University Press (Cambridge: 1978), p. 56. The real bills doctrine claims that borrowing can be divided into two types— borrowing used for productive uses and borrowing used for speculative uses. According to the doctrine, only the latter type can be inflationary.

[3] See Federal Reserve Act, Section 1-078.

[4] For more information, see CRS Report RS20826, *Structure and Functions of The Federal Reserve System*, by Pauline Smale.

[5] SeeCRS Report RL30354, *Monetary Policy and the Federal Reserve: Current Policy and Conditions*, by Gail E. Makinen and Marc Labonte.

[6] SeeCRS Report RL31325, *The Federal Migrant Education Program as Amended by the No Child Left Behind Act of 2001*, by Jeffrey J. Kuenzi.

[7] See CRS Report RL30344, *Inflation: Causes, Costs, and Current Status*, by Marc Labonte and Gail E. Makinen.

[8] See CRS Report RL31955, *Central Bank Independence and Economic Performance: What Does the Evidence Show?*, by Marc Labonte and Gail E. Makinen.

[9] Other reasons why monetary policy is preferred by economists include the fact that the Fed's staff is more specialized, the fact that monetary policy can be altered more quickly because it does not go through the legislative process, and because of exchange rate and interest rate benefits to using monetary policy rather than fiscal policy.

[10] For example, see Thomas Sargent, "The Ends of Four Big Inflations," in R. Hall, ed., *Inflation: Causes and Effects* (University of Chicago Press, 1982).

[11] Evaluations in this context should be distinguished from audit powers proposed for GAO in some proposals. Unlike the economic analysis performed by support agencies such as CBO or the Joint Tax Committee, audits of the type conducted by GAO are essentially checks of accounting and management procedures. Thus, granting of broader audit powers would not be expected to generate independent economic evaluations of Fed monetary policy.

[12] For more information on monetary policy rules, see CRS Report RL31050, *Formulation of Monetary Policy by the Federal Reserve: Rules vs. Discretion*, by Marc Labonte.

[13] For more information, see CRS Report 98-16, *Should the Federal Reserve Adopt an Inflation Target?*, by Marc Labonte and Gail E. Makinen and CRS Report RL31702, *Price Stability (Inflation Targeting) as the Sole Goal of Monetary Policy: The International Experience*, by Marc Labonte and Gail E. Makinen

[14] In this vein, the recent Japanese experience of prolonged deflation suggests that an inflation target should also have a lower boundary to prevent the persistence of poor policy in the other direction.

[15] Ben Bernanke and Frederic Mishkin, "Inflation Targeting: A New Framework for Monetary Policy?" *Journal of Economic Perspectives*, vol. 11, no. 2, spring 1997, p. 106.

[16] Milton Friedman, "An Independent Monetary Authority," in Leland Yeager, ed., *In Search of A Monetary Constitution* (Cambridge: Harvard University Press, 1962), p. 240.

In: The Federal Reserve
Editor: John P. Ranchett

ISBN: 978-1-62100-528-5
© 2011 Nova Science Publishers, Inc.

Chapter 4

CHANGING THE FEDERAL RESERVE'S MANDATE: AN ECONOMIC ANALYSIS[*]

Marc Labonte

SUMMARY

The Federal Reserve's (Fed's) current statutory mandate calls for it to "promote effectively the goals of maximum employment, stable prices, and moderate long-term interest rates." Some economists have argued that the current mandate should be replaced with a single mandate of price stability. Often the proposal for a single mandate is paired with a more specific proposal that the Fed should adopt an inflation target. Under an inflation target, the goal of monetary policy would be to achieve an explicit, numerical target or range for some measure of price inflation. Inflation targets could be required by Congress or voluntarily adopted by the Fed as a way to pursue price stability, or a single mandate could be adopted without an inflation target. Alternatively, an inflation target could be adopted under the current mandate.

For at least the past two decades, bills have been introduced in Congress to switch the Fed's current mandate to a single mandate of price stability. In the 112th Congress, Representative Pence introduced H.R. 245, which would strike the goal of maximum employment from the mandate; it does not include an inflation target. Were a single mandate to

---

[*] This is an edited, reformatted and augmented version of a Congressional Research Service publication, CRS Report for Congress R41656, from www.crs.gov, dated February 25, 2011.

be adopted in the United States, it would follow an international trend that has seen many foreign central banks adopt single mandates or inflation targets in recent decades.

Arguments made in favor of a price stability mandate are that it would better ensure that inflation was low and stable; increase predictability of monetary policy for financial markets; narrow the potential to pursue monetary policies with short-term political benefits but long-term costs; remove statutory goals that the Fed has no control over in the long run; limit policy discretion; and increase transparency, oversight, accountability, and credibility. Defenders of the current mandate argue that the Fed has already delivered low and stable inflation for the past two decades, unemployment is a valid statutory goal since it is influenced by monetary policy in the short run, and discretion is desirable to respond to unforeseen economic shocks. A case could also be made that changing the mandate alone would not significantly alter policymaking, because Fed discretion, transparency, oversight, and credibility are mostly influenced by other factors, such as the Fed's political independence.

Discontent with the Fed's performance in recent years has led to calls for legislative change. It is not clear that a single mandate would have altered its performance, however. Some of the criticisms, including lax regulation of banks and mortgages and "bailouts" of "too big to fail" firms, were authorized by statute unrelated to the Fed's monetary policy mandate. The criticism that the Fed was responsible for the depth and length of the recession leads to the prescription that monetary policy should have been more stimulative; it does not follow that more stimulus would have been pursued under a single mandate. Whether or not the Fed allowed the housing bubble to inflate, it is not clear that a single mandate would have changed matters since the housing bubble did not result in indisputably higher inflation. Some economists believe that the Fed's recent policy of "quantitative easing" (large-scale asset purchases) will result in high inflation. Since inflation has not increased to date, a single mandate would not have prevented quantitative easing. The Fed has discretion to pursue policies it believes are consistent with its mandate, and it has argued that quantitative easing was necessary to avoid price deflation. It could still make this argument under a single mandate.

This report discusses a number of implementation issues surrounding an inflation target. These include what rate of inflation to target, what inflation measure to use, whether to set a point target or range, and what penalties to impose if a target is missed.

INTRODUCTION

The recent financial crisis and deep economic recession have led to criticisms of the Federal Reserve's (Fed's) handling of both. Critics have blamed the Fed for pursuing policies that allowed the housing bubble to inflate, for lax regulation of financial firms and mortgage markets that led to excessive speculation, for "bailing out" financial firms during the crisis, for failing to prevent the recession's unusual length and depth, and for engaging in "quantitative easing" that critics believe will result in high inflation. Although alternative explanations have also been offered for each of these criticisms, they have led some Members of Congress to question whether legislative remedies are needed to avoid similar problems in the future. In particular, some Members of Congress have argued that the Fed's statutory mandate should be modified.

The Fed's statutory mandate was set in the "Federal Reserve Reform Act of 1977."[1] It currently reads:

> The Board of Governors of the Federal Reserve System and the Federal Open Market Committee shall maintain long run growth of the monetary and credit aggregates commensurate with the economy's long run potential to increase production, so as to promote effectively the goals of maximum employment, stable prices, and moderate longterm interest rates.[2]

Although this mandate includes three goals, it is often referred to by economists as a "dual mandate" of maximum employment and stable prices. Some economists have argued that Congress should strike the goals of maximum employment and moderate long-term interest rates from the current mandate, leaving price stability as the only mandated goal. Often the proposal for a single mandate is paired with a more specific proposal that the Fed should adopt an inflation target. Under an inflation target, the goal of monetary policy would aim to achieve a predefined numerical target or range for some measure of inflation (the change in the general price level).

For at least the past two decades, bills have been introduced in Congress to switch the Federal Reserve to a single mandate of price stability. In the 112th Congress, Representative Pence introduced H.R. 245 that would change the Fed's mandate to a single mandate of price stability; it does not include an inflation target. Were a single mandate to be adopted in the United States, it would follow an international trend that has seen many foreign central banks, including those of New Zealand, Canada, Australia, and the United Kingdom, adopt price stability mandates, inflation targets, or both in recent decades.

This report analyzes the economic arguments for and against shifting to a single mandate. It then analyzes possible effects of a mandate change on Fed policymaking in the context of recent criticisms related to the Fed's performance. It also discusses the advantages and disadvantages of different options for implementing an inflation target.

BACKGROUND ON MONETARY POLICY

Congress has delegated monetary policy responsibilities to the Fed, and requires the Fed to set monetary policy to achieve its mandated goals. In normal circumstances, the Fed implements monetary policy by setting a target for the federal funds rate, the overnight inter-bank lending rate. (During the recent financial crisis, the Fed has taken several unconventional steps to stimulate economic activity besides changes in the federal funds target.[3]) Generally, if the Fed wishes to moderate the growth in economic output and inflationary pressures, it "tightens" or "contracts" policy by raising the federal funds target. If it wishes to stimulate the growth in economic output and inflationary pressures, it "loosens" or "expands" policy by reducing the federal funds rate.

Congress has given the Fed broad day-to-day discretion to choose the federal funds rate target that the Fed believes is compatible with its statutory goals. Congress retains oversight responsibilities, and those responsibilities are primarily exercised through Congressional hearings, including mandated semi-annual hearings in which the committees of jurisdiction receive a written report and testimony from the Chairman of the Fed. If Congress finds the Fed's pursuit of its statutory goals to be lacking, however, it has limited "carrots" or "sticks" available to induce a change in behavior. A fundamental problem with holding the Fed accountable for its performance is that it has a limited influence over economic outcomes. When the actual performance of the economy deviates from the mandated goals, the Fed can make the case, with some justification, that those deviations were caused by factors outside of its control.

Monetary policy is only one of the Fed's main responsibilities. Other responsibilities—including lender of last resort functions in a crisis and supervision of banks and the payment system—are laid out in other sections of the Federal Reserve Act and other parts of federal statute. Changing the Fed's monetary policy mandate alone would not alter the authorities governing the Fed's other responsibilities.

THE RELATIONSHIP BETWEEN INFLATION TARGETING AND THE MANDATE

The statutory mandate sets the ultimate goals of monetary policy, and can be altered only through legislative action. The instruments, methods, and strategies that the Fed employs to reach those goals is not laid out in law. Inflation targeting can be thought of as a strategy for achieving mandated goals—direct policy at achieving a numerical target for inflation. Because it is a strategy for achieving statutory goals, it could be codified through legislation or adopted internally by the Fed.

Traditionally, proponents of a single mandate and inflation targeting have been one and the same. There is logic to the idea that if the Fed's sole focus of policy is going to be achieving price stability, then there should be a numerical target to help ensure that goal is achieved and facilitate evaluation of the Fed's performance in relation to the mandate. Legislation could include both, but need not. One might favor a single mandate of price stability, but oppose a legislated inflation target on the grounds that the Fed should have maximum independence and flexibility to pursue that mandate. Or Congress might legislate a single mandate, and the Fed could then choose whether to voluntarily adopt an inflation target to help meet the single mandate.

Although many proponents of inflation targeting also favor a single mandate, an inflation target could also be adopted without changing the current mandate. Fed Chairman Ben Bernanke was a well-known advocate of inflation targeting before his time at the Fed, but has repeatedly defended the dual mandate in its current form while at the Fed. He has suggested that an inflation target would be complementary to the dual mandate. In 2005, he testified:

> One possible step toward greater transparency would be for the FOMC to state explicitly the numerical inflation rate or range of inflation rates it considers to be consistent with the goal of long-term price stability, a practice currently employed by many of the world's central banks. I have supported this idea in my academic writings and in speeches as a board member. Providing quantitative guidance about the meaning of "long-term price stability" could have several advantages,

including further reducing public uncertainty about monetary policy and anchoring long-term inflation expectations even more effectively. I view the explicit statement of a long-run inflation objective as fully consistent with the Federal Reserve's current policy approach, including its appropriate emphasis on the role of judgment and flexibility in policymaking. Most important, this step would in no way reduce the importance of maximum employment as a policy goal. Indeed, a key justification for this action is its potential to contribute to stronger and more stable employment growth by further stabilizing inflation and inflation expectations.[4]

Although it is debatable whether an inflation target is compatible with the equal weighting of maximum employment and price stability in the dual mandate, given the Fed's broad discretion over policy implementation, the Fed would not need to seek new authority or wait for a mandate change to adopt an inflation target if it desired.

EVALUATING THE RATIONALES FOR A SINGLE MANDATE OF PRICE STABILITY

Proponents claim that a series of related benefits would stem from a single mandate of price stability. These claims have been criticized on two grounds— that purported benefits would actually result in worse policy and economic outcomes than the status quo, or that the Fed, in practice, has already delivered the same benefits under the current dual mandate. In fact, some economists have referred to the Fed as an "implicit inflation targeter" because of the latter argument.[5] This section considers each of those arguments in turn.[6]

For clarity of discussion, this report will treat a single mandate and inflation targeting as complementary when evaluating the merits and drawbacks of the proposal unless otherwise noted. In other words, an inflation target would increase the benefits and drawbacks of changing the mandate. It should be noted, however, that more of the literature has focused on inflation targeting than on a single mandate, so certain authors may not necessarily have intended their arguments to be applied to both.

The Level and Stability of Price Inflation

A long-standing critique of macroeconomic policymakers is that they inappropriately choose the short-term political benefits of low unemployment over the long-term costs of higher inflation. Election-minded policymakers allegedly have a bias toward overly stimulative policy in an effort to "rev up" the economy beyond its sustainable limits that ultimately results in undesirably high inflation beyond their political horizons. While the dual mandate already calls for stable prices, its inclusion of maximum employment could potentially allow policymakers to justify this bias. Proponents of a single mandate claim that it would reduce the scope for policymakers to indulge in that bias, and would therefore result in lower and more stable inflation over time.

Two questions can be answered with empirical evidence to help evaluate the legitimacy of this argument. First, has the Fed consistently delivered price stability under a dual mandate? Second, have other countries with single mandates or inflation targets delivered low and stable inflation more consistently than the Fed?

Although inflation was high in the 1970s and parts of the 1980s, it has been consistently low and stable, as measured by the consumer price index (CPI), over the past two decades. The increase in the overall CPI has been below 4% for the year in each year since 1991.[7] In its policymaking, the Fed has preferred to focus on core inflation, which omits food and energy prices. Using the Fed's preferred measure, the core CPI has been above 1% and below 3% each year since 1995 and has not shown any tendency to rise at the end of the past two business cycles. In other words, the Fed has been highly successful at achieving price stability by its preferred measure for 15 years, and almost as successful by a broader measure of inflation.[8] (House prices are not included in any of the common measures of price inflation, so the rapid increase in house prices in the 2000s had no direct effect on inflation.)

Some economists believe that the Fed has pursued policies since the financial crisis that are incompatible with price stability, but those unconventional policies have not, to date, resulted in any tangible increase in inflation.[9] The Fed, for its part, has argued that those policies are necessary for price stability, in order to avoid price deflation.

Further, the Fed's inflation record is not significantly different from that of major inflation targeters.[10] For example, from 2000 to 2010, average inflation in the United States was within one percentage point of the average for major inflation targeters, with inflation in Australia and New Zealand slightly higher than the United States, and inflation in the Euro Area, United Kingdom, and Canada slightly lower.[11]

There has been some dispute among economists as to whether overall inflation or a core measure is a more appropriate benchmark for evaluating the Fed's performance.[12] But in the context of changing the mandate, two points can be made. First, the Fed's record on price stability by its preferred measure over the last 15 years could not have been improved upon under an alternate mandate or an inflation target. Second, its record is not quite as good by other measures. But if one believes that the Fed is defining price stability incorrectly (e.g., it should use overall inflation instead of core inflation, or it should include house prices in its inflation measure), one would have to explicitly add that to a mandate change or inflation target. Otherwise, the Fed would have discretion to define price stability in terms of whatever measure it prefers.

The Fed's record on inflation may be good, contrary to the predicted policy bias, because the Fed's independence may already be sufficient to allow it to effectively ignore short-term benefits of higher inflation. In other words, a mandate change is not necessary for the Fed to resist the temptation to pursue policies with short-term benefits and long-term costs.

The Long-Run Neutrality of Money on Employment

A central tenet of mainstream economic theory is that money is neutral in the long run, meaning that changes in monetary policy do not have permanent effects on the level of employment. In the long run, it is primarily labor market policy that influences the "natural rate" of unemployment, and the Fed has no control over labor market policy.[13] (The mandate's call for "maximum employment" is typically interpreted to mean keeping unemployment near its natural rate, as opposed to, say, reducing unemployment to zero.)

Proponents of a mandate change argue that the Fed's mandate should not include a variable that the Fed cannot control in the long run. Further, some economists have argued that the best way for the Fed to contribute to economic efficiency in the long run is by keeping prices stable.[14] Price stability reduces errors made by economic agents because of mistaken forecasts about future price movements, and reduces "shoe leather" costs caused by the expense and effort of individuals to protect themselves against inflation.[15]

While a belief that monetary policy has no long-term effect on employment may be fairly uncontroversial, it is also uncontroversial to assert that monetary policy has a significant effect on the business cycle, which is the main driver of total employment and unemployment in the short run. It can take several years for the economy to return to full employment after a downturn, and the economy rarely remains at full employment for long. In economist Olivier Blanchard's view, "while money is eventually neutral...monetary policy can affect the real interest rate for a decade and perhaps more...[and] output or unemployment, for a roughly equal time..."[16] Thus, as a practical matter, the effect of monetary policy on employment is always a relevant policy concern. Foreign central banks with single mandates have proven to still adjust monetary policy in response to changes in employment, in practice.

Some would also question the mainstream premise that monetary policy has no long-term effect on employment. A central tenet to the natural rate of unemployment concept is that the natural rate is unaffected by the business cycle. There is a theory, called "hysteresis," that prolonged periods of high unemployment raise the natural rate of unemployment. This could occur, for example, because a worker's skills are eroded by episodes of long-term unemployment, making the individual less employable when the economy recovers. If the hysteresis argument is correct, monetary policy could influence employment in the long run. For example, an aggressively stimulative monetary policy could prevent hysteresis by limiting long-term unemployment following a deep recession. Such a policy might be more aggressive than what would be called for solely on the basis of maintaining price stability. Policymakers would have to decide where to draw the line in the tradeoff between combating hysteresis and maintaining price stability, but this is in contrast with the neutrality of money argument that there is no long-term tradeoff.

Stagflation: The Proper Response when Mandated Goals Diverge

One criticism of the dual mandate is that the Fed has multiple goals, but only one instrument (open market operations) to pursue those goals. When goals conflict, the mandate offers no guidance as to which goal takes precedence.

Most of the time, employment and inflation move together. During economic downturns, employment and inflation both decline; during booms, they both rise. In those cases, the policy prescription is likely to be the same—

expansionary in a boom and contractionary in a downturn—under a single or dual mandate. For example, the Fed is currently concerned that employment and inflation are too low—in these circumstances, both a single or dual mandate would call for expansionary policy. Further, movements in employment are seen as leading indicators of future movements in inflation. If that is the case, monetary policy would respond to movements in employment even if policymakers were only concerned with price stability. It follows that, in normal circumstances, policy reactions to changes in employment would be similar under a single or dual mandate.

There are cases when employment and inflation do not move together, however. For example, "supply shocks," such as a sharp increase in the price of oil, would temporarily reduce economic activity while temporarily increasing inflation. The most famous case is the "stagflation" of the 1970s, when the recessions beginning in 1973 and 1979 both involved rising inflation and falling employment. High inflation persisted throughout the 1970s and was not wrung out of the system until a second, deeper recession occurred beginning in 1981. If stagflation occurred, tighter or easier monetary policy would be consistent with the dual mandate, whereas the single mandate would call for neutral or tighter policy (if the supply shock caused all prices to begin rising more rapidly). For many economists who have supported a single mandate, the poor performance of the 1970s is the main argument in favor of changing the mandate (although the dual mandate was not adopted until 1978). The argument against easing policy during stagflation would be that, if one accepts the premise that monetary policy has no long-term effects on employment, the efficiency gains of price stability outweigh the short-term costs of temporarily higher unemployment. While that may be the case, to some policymakers, the long-term benefits of lower inflation would not outweigh the short-term costs of high unemployment.

Transparency and Discretion

Proponents of a single mandate argue that it would improve monetary policy by reducing the Fed's policymaking discretion. The result of a broad mandate, they argue, is that the Fed does not have to offer any systematic rationale for its policy decisions, and can therefore pursue any policy direction it desires. Sometimes monetary policy is criticized for excessive "fine tuning," meaning the adjustment of policy to every small economic development, which some economists believe is in itself destabilizing. It is argued that a more hands-off approach would reduce the volatility in economic growth and prices.

Discretion, they argue, also reduces transparency, meaning, in this context, the ability of market participants to predict and comprehend the rationale of monetary policy changes. A better understanding of monetary policy makes it more effective, it is argued, by improving the accuracy and ability of the private sector's economic planning. An inflation target, for example, might make it clearer to market participants what the Fed's plans were and what goals it was trying to accomplish. Proponents do not claim that the Fed would lose all discretion under a single mandate, but have sometimes described inflation targeting as "constrained discretion."[17]

Other economists argue that maximum discretion is necessary and desirable because short-term economic performance is dominated by unforeseen shocks, and it is these shocks, rather than policy mistakes, that are the root cause of economic volatility. Were policymakers not free to rapidly respond to those shocks, they believe, downturns would be deeper and more frequent. Since these shocks affect recorded inflation with a long lag, if policymakers felt compelled under a single mandate or inflation target to wait until prices had changed to respond, then the response could be undesirably late. For example, inflation (as measured by the CPI) in 2008 rose 3.8%, which was its highest rate since 1991. If the Fed had felt compelled to focus policy solely on the inflation rate, it might have felt constrained in its response to the financial crisis that occurred that year. Flexibility allowed the Fed to introduce multiple innovative and unconventional policies to respond to problems in financial markets as they arose during the crisis.

An alternative perspective is that a single mandate alone would do little to curb the Fed's discretion because its discretion flows mainly from other sources, primarily the Fed's high degree of independence from Congress and Congress's longstanding custom of not involving itself in the Fed's day-to-day policymaking decisions. There is no outside arbiter to deem whether the Fed's decisions are consistent with its mandate now, and that would still be the case if the mandate were changed in isolation. In this light, the Fed's discretionary powers would not be significantly affected by a change in the mandate, but could be affected by other provisions that accompany a mandate change in legislation. For example, an inflation target could reduce the Fed's discretion by reducing the scope for policy options that would cause inflation to miss its target, although the extent that a target would reduce discretion depends greatly on the design of the target, as discussed below. But even the breaching of an inflation target would not trigger any automatic change in policy, as they have operated in other countries.[18]

An argument could also be made that a single mandate would not greatly alter the Fed's transparency, in the sense of the term as used in this section, because the Fed is already highly transparent. It releases quarterly economic forecasts. Minutes of Federal Open Market Committee meetings are released with a lag. Typically, changes in interest rates and other policy decisions are well predicted and expected by market participants before they occur. Transparency flows primarily from the Fed's communication style—major policy changes are typically hinted at and debated in speeches, interviews, or articles by Fed officials before they are announced. Since current transparency practices are largely voluntary, they may be unaffected by a mandate change.

Oversight and Accountability

A criticism of the current mandate has been that the multiple statutory goals are so broad and wide-ranging that they can be used to justify virtually any policy decision. Critics say that this makes effective Congressional oversight difficult, and makes the Fed unaccountable for policy mistakes. Oversight and accountability would improve under a single mandate, according to proponents, because it would make it easier to evaluate the Fed's performance, particularly if the single mandate included an inflation target.

Congress has considerable scope to alter the degree of accountability that is unrelated to the mandate, however. For example, it controls the number of hearings and Government Accountability Office audits on Federal Reserve issues, as well as the number of reports that it requires the Fed to produce for it. Accountability may be hampered mainly by two other factors that a single mandate does not address.

First, the functioning of the economy is complex, and Congress may lack the specialization to independently assess the Fed's performance. For example, the Fed does not typically refer to its dual mandate to justify bad economic outcomes—it blames them on factors outside its control. Since the Fed's influence on the economy is limited, it is certainly the case that many of the negative shocks that influence the economy could not be prevented by the Fed. But for effective accountability, Congress must be able to effectively determine whether bad economic outcomes (such as missing an inflation target) are caused by the Fed or beyond the Fed's control.

Second, there are many institutional factors that make the Fed less accountable than a typical executive branch agency. There are no statutory or institutional consequences for missing the mandated goals; nor is there any formal process for identifying when the goals have been missed. The Fed's officials do not answer to the President. Fed governors are appointed to long, overlapping terms. The Fed is self-funded and is not subject to the appropriation process or any other form of regular Congressional budgetary review. By statute, the Government Accountability Office cannot perform monetary policy evaluations of the Fed. There are statutory barriers to its interaction with the executive branch—for example, it cannot purchase federal debt directly from the Treasury. While all of these factors make the Fed less accountable, they also make the Fed more independent from Congress. Many economists have argued that this independence is desirable because it is responsible for the Fed's overall record of good policymaking.

Credibility

Another argument made in favor of a single mandate is that it will enhance the Fed's credibility, and monetary policy is more effective under credible central banks. In a well-known paper, economist Kenneth Rogoff argued that if a central bank has a reputation of being tough on inflation, then when the central bank eases policy, it will be more effective than if the central bank lacked credibility.[19] This phenomenon can be illustrated by looking at monetary policy's effect on interest rates across the yield curve. Stimulative monetary policy involves reducing short-term interest rates, but economic activity may be more responsive to changes in long-term interest rates. If a central bank lacking credibility reduces interest rates, markets may believe that it will lead to high inflation in the future, which could prevent long-term interest rates from falling. But when a credible central bank reduces short-term rates, long-term rates could follow since there are less fears of inflation.

There does not appear to be compelling evidence at this time that the Fed suffers from a lack of credibility with market participants. Inflation expectations are low despite the fact that the Fed is currently pursuing an unconventional policy that, under normal circumstances, would be inconsistent with price stability. Long-term interest rates are at low levels by historical standards. Foreigners continue to be willing to hold U.S. assets. Thus, the Fed may gain little additional credibility from a switch to a single mandate.

RECENT CRITICISMS OF THE FED'S PERFORMANCE: WOULD A SINGLE MANDATE HAVE RESULTED IN BETTER OUTCOMES?

Since the financial crisis began, the Fed has been subject to significant criticism on a number of different fronts. Some would argue that its shortcomings of the past few years are a sign that legislative action is needed to improve its performance. This section analyzes whether a switch to a single mandate might have altered the criticized policy decisions.

The Length and Depth of the Recession

The Fed has been criticized for not preventing the last recession from becoming the longest and deepest recession since the Great Depression. In this sense, the Fed failed to fulfill its dual mandate, although economists are divided about how much factors beyond the Fed's control are to blame. What is difficult to dispute is that beginning in August 2007—months before the recession officially began—the Fed undertook a series of aggressive steps to stimulate the economy and provide liquidity to the financial sector. These steps were innovative and unconventional, and included reducing short-term interest rates to nearly zero, creating a series of unprecedented lending facilities, and conducting "quantitative easing" (large-scale purchases of securities, including mortgage-backed securities).[20] While there has been criticism of the longterm implications of some of these policy steps, it is difficult to argue that the Fed was too passive in responding to the recession. For critics of unconventional policy, constraint would have been desirable from a long-term perspective, but in the short run, a less aggressive policy would have resulted in less monetary stimulus, and probably a deeper and longer recession.

Further, it is not clear how the Fed would have acted differently under a single mandate or an inflation target. The Fed's unconventional policy initiatives were not required to be justified in terms of its mandate. It can be argued that many of these initiatives were undertaken under the Fed's lender of last resort duties, which are not contained within its mandate.[21] Several initiatives relied on the Fed's emergency lending powers, which are found in a separate part of the Federal Reserve Act, Section 13(3). Perhaps the Fed would have felt constrained to act less aggressively during the crisis if inflation had been above its target, although the Fed might have justified its actions by arguing that the crisis made deflation a greater threat than inflation.

The Housing Bubble

A separate criticism is that the underlying cause of the recession was the growth and subsequent bursting of the housing bubble, which led to crippling losses in the financial sector that eventually led to panic. Some critics have argued that the Fed should have prevented the housing bubble from inflating in the first place; if it had done so, then the bursting of the bubble would not have been so damaging to the financial system and economy. These critics argue that the Fed left stimulative monetary policy in place for too long after the 2001 recession, and the resulting low mortgage rates helped inflate the bubble. For example, the federal funds target was 2% or less until December 2004, three years after the recession had ended. These critics argue that the Fed should have raised interest rates to cool down the housing market when house prices started to accelerate.[22]

Chairman Bernanke has argued that

> Even if monetary policy was not a principal cause of the housing bubble, some have argued that the Fed could have stopped the bubble at an earlier stage by more-aggressive interest rate increases. For several reasons, this was not a practical policy option. First, in 2003 or so, when the policy rate was at its lowest level, there was little agreement about whether the increase in housing prices was a bubble or not (or, a popular hypothesis, that there was a bubble but that it was restricted to certain parts of the country). Second, and more important, monetary policy is a blunt tool; raising the general level of interest rates to manage a single asset price would undoubtedly have had large side effects on other assets and sectors of the economy. In this case, to significantly affect monthly payments and other measures of housing affordability, the FOMC likely would have had to increase interest rates quite sharply, at a time when the recovery was viewed as "jobless" and deflation was perceived as a threat.[23]

For the purposes of this report, it is not necessary to settle the debate about whether the Fed should be blamed for the housing bubble. Rather, the relevant question is whether a single mandate or inflation target would have led the Fed to tighten policy sooner to avoid a bubble. Quotes from Chairman Bernanke suggest that this is unlikely. Chairman Bernanke has stated that, even in hindsight, "...monetary policy from 2002 to 2006 appears to have been reasonably consistent with the Federal Reserve's mandated goals of maximum sustainable employment and price stability..."[24] He has also said, before the financial crisis, that

> ...to the extent that a stock-market boom causes, or simply forecasts, sharply higher spending on consumer goods and new capital, it may indicate incipient inflationary pressures. Policy tightening might therefore be called for—but to contain the incipient inflation not to arrest the stock-market boom per se.[25]

Neither the dot-com bubble nor the housing bubble was manifested in high overall price inflation, so a single mandate is unlikely to have made the Fed more responsive to those bubbles than the dual mandate.

Asset bubbles are likely to continue to be a policy concern in the future. If policymakers believe the Fed should be more responsive to future asset bubbles, they could instead expand the mandate to require that the Fed prevent asset bubbles or, more generally, ensure financial stability.[26]

Quantitative Easing

Some economists have criticized the Fed's decision to pursue "quantitative easing" (expansion in the Fed's balance sheet through large-scale asset purchases)[27] on the grounds that it will lead to high inflation.[28] In normal conditions, extended quantitative easing would be inconsistent with price stability, but the Fed believes that because of problems in the economy and financial markets, quantitative easing is needed for a timely economic recovery and to reduce the threat of deflation. The Fed also believes that quantitative easing will support mortgage markets and assist a recovery in the housing market.

The link between quantitative easing and price stability is clearer than the link between the other recent criticisms of the Fed. Nevertheless, as long as the Fed is given discretion to pursue policies that it believes are consistent with price stability, it seems doubtful that a single mandate would have prevented the Fed from pursuing price stability. This can be demonstrated by examining the following FOMC statement announcing the first round of large-scale asset purchases:

> In light of increasing economic slack here and abroad, the Committee expects that inflation will remain subdued. Moreover, the Committee sees some risk that inflation could persist for a time below rates that best foster economic growth and price stability in the longer term.
>
> In these circumstances, the Federal Reserve will employ all available tools to promote economic recovery and to preserve price stability.... To provide greater support to mortgage lending and housing markets, the Committee decided today to increase the size of the Federal Reserve's balance sheet further by purchasing up to an additional $750 billion of agency mortgage-backed securities, bringing its total purchases of these securities to up to $1.25 trillion this year, and to increase its purchases of agency debt this year by up to $100 billion to a total of up to $200 billion. Moreover, to help improve conditions in private credit markets, the Committee decided to purchase up to $300 billion of longer-term Treasury securities over the next six months.[29]

Similarly, the November 2010 FOMC announcement of another round of asset purchases, popularly coined "quantitative easing 2," reads:

> To promote a stronger pace of economic recovery and to help ensure that inflation, over time, is at levels consistent with its mandate, the Committee decided today to expand its holdings of securities.... the Committee intends to purchase a further $600 billion of longer-term Treasury securities by the end of the second quarter of 2011, a pace of about $75 billion per month. The Committee will regularly review the pace of its securities purchases and the overall size of the asset-purchase program in light of incoming information and will adjust the program as needed to best foster maximum employment and price stability.[30]

In both of these announcements, the Fed justified its decisions in terms of the need to avoid deflation in order to achieve price stability under the dual mandate. Switching to a single mandate would presumably not change the Fed's belief that quantitative easing is necessary to maintain price stability.

A related fear raised by some is that the Fed is "monetizing the federal debt" through quantitative easing, meaning that the Fed is financing the government's budget deficits. Direct purchase of the debt from the Treasury by the Fed is already forbidden under Section 14 of the Federal Reserve Act, and would thus not be affected by a mandate change. The authority to purchase Treasury securities in the secondary market is also found in Section 14 of the act.

Failure to Respond to Rising Headline Inflation

As measured by the consumer price index, overall (referred to as "headline") inflation has been lower on average since 1992 than it had been since the mid-1960s. Although the Fed's record in this regard is very good, a case could nevertheless be made that the Fed should focus more on headline inflation and less on core inflation, particularly since headline inflation has outpaced core inflation in 10 of the past 12 years. One criticism that could be leveled at the Fed is that headline inflation rose above 3% before the last two recessions, and the Fed was too slow to respond at the expense of price stability and economic stability. The increase in overall inflation that preceded the last two recessions may suggest to some that there were important signals that the economy was overheating that the Fed may have neglected because of its focus on core inflation. Core CPI stayed below 3% before the two previous recessions.

The rationale for focusing on core inflation is that it is more representative of underlying inflationary pressures because it leaves out two highly volatile components, these being food and energy. A focus on increases in inflation caused by transitory movements in volatile components of the CPI could result in "false positives," leading to changes in interest rates when underlying inflationary pressures have not really changed. Headline inflation has generally outpaced core in recent years because commodity prices have tended to rise more rapidly than other prices, but it is not clear that this trend will continue in the future.

If it is believed that the Fed's focus on core inflation has led to poor policymaking, switching to a single mandate alone would arguably do little to solve the problem. As long as the Fed retained discretion to define price stability, it could continue to define price stability in terms of the performance of core inflation, or any other measure it favored. If an inflation target were adopted, any potential policy shift on this issue would depend on whether headline or core inflation were targeted.

"Bailing out" too Big to Fail Firms

In 2008, the Fed intervened financially to prevent two large financial firms, Bear Stearns and American International Group (AIG), from failing on the grounds that they were "too big to fail."[31] In other words, the Fed believed their failure would have undermined the stability of the financial system as a whole. Many critics have argued that these interventions increase risk in the financial system in the long run by increasing "moral hazard," meaning that anticipated rescue from bad outcomes leads to greater risk taking.

The Fed also provided liquidity through a series of newly-created, broadly-based lending facilities to non-bank financial firms, such as primary dealers. Some critics argue that the Fed should not have provided assistance to firms that it did not regulate for safety and soundness, since the Fed cannot mitigate moral hazard at firms it does not regulate. Until 2010, the Fed regulated only bank holding companies, financial holding companies, domestic branches of foreign banks, and state-chartered member banks.

For both the assistance to AIG and Bear Stearns and the broadly-based facilities, the Fed provided assistance primarily through its emergency lending authority, found in Section 13(3) of the Federal Reserve Act. That authority was amended by The Dodd-Frank Wall Street Reform and Consumer Protection Act (P.L. 111-203), which attempted to prohibit future "bail outs" of failing firms, while allowing the Fed to set up broadly-based emergency liquidity facilities. Some critics felt that the Fed's emergency lending authority should be repealed or further restricted, but a change in the Fed's monetary policy mandate would not affect this authority.

Lax Supervision of the Financial System and Mortgage Markets

Some economists believe a root cause of the financial crisis was excessive risk-taking by financial firms. When risks were realized, these both contributed to the general panic and left those firms unable to survive the panic without government assistance. Some—but not all—of the firms that relied on Federal Reserve lending emergency facilities during the crisis were bank holding companies that were regulated by the Fed for safety and soundness. If the Fed had required these firms to take steps such as hold more capital or greater liquidity, the firms may have fared better in the crisis. The Fed is also accused of having failed to anticipate the problems that led to and exacerbated the crisis until it was too late.

The Fed also had regulatory responsibility for consumer products, such as mortgages. Critics argue that the housing bubble could have been avoided had the Fed used its consumer protection powers to prevent people from taking out unsuitable mortgages. A number of non-traditional mortgage products have proven in hindsight to have high default rates, and many of these products allowed borrowers to borrow more than they would have been eligible to with traditional products. It is argued that house prices could not have risen so quickly without the growth in nontraditional products.

Chairman Bernanke has admitted that the Fed and other regulators should have done more to protect consumers against unsuitable mortgages. He said

> The Federal Reserve and other agencies did make efforts to address poor mortgage underwriting practices.... However, these efforts came too late or were insufficient to stop the decline in underwriting standards and effectively constrain the housing bubble.[32]

The Fed's failure to prevent the crisis was not unique—domestic firms regulated by other regulators, foreign firms regulated by foreign regulators, and domestic firms that were not regulated for safety and soundness all experienced liquidity or solvency problems during the crisis. Few policymakers, investors, or academics accurately anticipated the problems that would arise from 2007 on.

The Fed's regulatory powers are not mentioned in its statutory mandate, and would not be affected by a change to a single monetary policy mandate. Its authority to regulate financial institutions for safety and soundness are found in Section 21 of the Federal Reserve Act and other parts of the U.S. Code. Its consumer protection responsibilities were not part of the original Federal Reserve Act, and were enumerated in a series of later acts. As a result of the Dodd-Frank Wall Street Reform and Consumer Protection Act (P.L. 111-203), the Fed's general consumer protection responsibilities have been reassigned to a new Consumer Financial Protection Bureau, housed in the Fed.

SETTING AN INFLATION TARGET: IMPLEMENTATION ISSUES

If Congress decided to legislate an inflation target, or the Fed decided to adopt one voluntarily, there are a number of institutional details to consider surrounding its scope and composition. Arguably, these issues would have important ramifications for economic and policy outcomes, as well as the scope of the Fed's discretion.[33]

Who Should Set the Inflation Target?

As discussed above, Congress could require an inflation target in statute, or leave it to the Fed to decide whether or not to adopt one. In addition, if Congress decided to require a target by statute, it could choose to set some of the parameters of that target in law or leave it to the Fed to set the parameters. Those parameters, discussed in the following sections, include the level of inflation to target, the price index to use for the target, whether to base the target on actual outcomes or forecasted outcomes, whether to target a point estimate or a band, and whether there should be penalties for missing the target. Any parameter that was set in law would be more difficult to change than if it were set by the Fed, for better or for worse.[34]

The consequence of setting the target and its attributes in law is that it would eliminate some of the Fed's discretion and accountability. As discussed above, for some policymakers, this would be a benefit as they believe that the discretion increases the risk of bad economic outcomes. For others, it would be a drawback, because some flexibility is desirable to deal with unexpected economic developments and contingencies.

What Level Should be Targeted?

The first question regarding an inflation target is what rate of inflation is consistent with price stability? Taken literally, price stability might be understood to be an inflation rate of 0%, but this would be quite a departure from post-World War II history, when inflation has never remained below 1% for more than a few months at a time. A 0% inflation rate would minimize the "menu costs" associated with inflation which refers to the costs firms have to incur to respond to nominal price changes, such as a restaurant that must reprint menus. But since inflation will sometimes miss its target because of unexpected shocks, a zero percent target makes it more likely that the economy would sometimes experience deflation. Furthermore, getting to zero inflation, when households and investors have long-standing expectations that inflation will be positive, could require a short-term slowdown in the economy.

An alternative definition offered by Alan Greenspan is that "price stability is best thought of as an environment in which inflation is so low and stable over time that it does not materially enter into the decisions of households and firms."[35] By this definition, the FOMC's long-run range for inflation of 1.5%

to 2% might be considered price stability. Since measures of inflation such as the CPI are believed to overstate the "true" inflation rate, a low but positive rate of measured inflation may be equivalent to true price stability.

An alternative view is that a little inflation, say 4%, can "grease the wheels" of the labor market.[36] This view is based on the claim that workers are less willing in the short run to accept a nominal wage cut than the equivalent real wage cut if it contains a nominal wage increase. For example, workers would be less willing to accept a 2% wage *cut* when inflation is zero than a 2% wage *increase* when inflation is 4%, even though the two options are equivalent in terms of purchasing power. In other words, workers suffer from "money illusion"—a proposition that many economists reject. If this is true, then the labor market would clear faster, meaning real wages would fall faster when unemployment was high, and the economy would return to full employment faster with a little inflation. A higher average rate of inflation would also reduce the likelihood of swings into price deflation during recessions and give conventional monetary policy more room to stimulate before it hits the "zero bound" on interest rates.[37] This would have to be balanced against the higher costs, such as menu costs, associated with moderately higher inflation.

Some economists have argued that the level of prices (price index) should be targeted instead of the inflation rate (change in prices). They argue that this would lead to less uncertainty about the future path of prices, which would aid businesses with their planning, for example. On the other hand, targeting the price level could arguably be destabilizing since policy would have to compensate after unexpected "price shocks." For example, if prices exceeded the targeted level by 2% in the first year, prices would have to fall by 2% relative to the baseline in future years to return to the targeted path of prices. It is not clear that the short-term cost of creating higher inflation or deflation to return to the planned price level path is worth the benefits. By contrast, if inflation were targeted and exceeded the target, "bygones would be bygones" in future years. In practice, countries that have adopted inflation targets typically target inflation, not the price level.

A Point Estimate or a Range?

Another choice in the design of an inflation target is whether the target should be a point estimate, such as 2%, or a range, such as between 1%-3%. If a range were chosen, policymakers would also need to decide whether the midpoint of the range was most desirable, or if hitting any part of the range is equally acceptable.

Because monetary policy only indirectly influences inflation in the short run, and inflation is influenced by unexpected shocks, actual inflation is unlikely to often hit a point estimate exactly. This distinction is less important if it is implicitly understood that small deviations from the point estimate are acceptable. A range would make the tolerance of small deviations explicit, and make misses due to unexpected events less frequent. On the other hand, if unexpected shocks are large, then to make the range wide enough to never miss the target due to unexpected shocks could render the target meaningless.

If actual inflation were targeted, a range would be more transparent, since deviations are unavoidable and the amount of tolerable deviation would be explicit. If future inflation were targeted, a point estimate might be more appropriate since the goal of policy is to achieve some specific future goal, even though forecast error means the goal will rarely ever be hit precisely.

What Measure of Inflation Should be Targeted?

Separate from the question of what numerical value should be targeted is the question of what data source should be used for the target. This question, which is important for accountability reasons, raises a number of issues. First, there are several official measures of inflation. The Bureau of Labor Statistics issues multiple measures of inflation, and the Bureau of Economic Analysis (BEA) issues several more, but a target would be based on just one. Should the inflation target be based on the change in the prices of all goods in the economy, the change in the price of consumer goods, or the change in wages? The best known measure of inflation is arguably the headline CPI, but a drawback of the CPI is that it is thought to overstate inflation because of some methodological problems. Familiarity may be a benefit at first, but wane in importance once the targeted measure becomes well known. The GDP deflator issued by BEA is the broadest measure of inflation. On the other hand, the measures issued by BEA are only released quarterly and are subject to data revisions—two characteristics that some consider less desirable for an inflation target.

Assuming the selected measure of inflation is based on the price of goods, a further issue is whether volatile elements of the price index should be omitted from the target. In other words, should core or headline inflation be targeted? If core is targeted, how many items should be omitted? Traditionally, core inflation is measured by omitting food and energy prices, but economists have also devised other measures of core inflation that they believe to have more desirable qualities.[38]

The benefit of using core inflation as a target is that removing volatile components of the inflation rate would make it less likely that the Fed would miss its target at any given time. It would also make it less likely that policy would be altered in response to transitory price changes. The drawback, as discussed above, is that targeting core inflation can lead to suboptimal performance if headline outpaces core for extended periods of time. An alternative approach to addressing price volatility would be to target overall inflation, but allow exceptions for unusual circumstances, such as an energy price spike. But too many exceptions could result in a level of discretion, accountability, and transparency that, in practice, was indistinguishable from current policy.

A final issue is whether recent (actual) inflation or future (forecasted) inflation should be targeted. Because monetary policy affects inflation only indirectly in the short run, and unexpected shocks often throw inflation off its expected path, the drawback to targeting actual inflation is that actual inflation will inevitably miss its target frequently. The other drawback to targeting actual inflation is that monetary policy affects inflation with lags. Inflation may be above the target in the period that has just occurred but be projected to fall below the target in the near future. If the Fed were responding to actual inflation, it may feel compelled to raise rates in this example, even though projections call for lower rates for the period that current monetary policy changes would influence. This hypothetical case is likely to be important in reality since inflation tends to peak right before the onset of a recession.

The drawback to targeting future inflation is that it would reduce transparency and accountability, particularly if the Fed were responsible for forecasting the inflation it was also targeting. There could be little consequence for actual inflation missing its target chronically, as long as the Fed produced forecasts that showed that it would meet the target in the future. It would be more difficult to apply any penalties (discussed below) to a regime based on targeting future inflation since the Fed would control the performance metric. Accountability might revolve less around why actual outcomes differed from desired outcomes and more around whether the Fed's forecasting was accurate, which could be difficult for Congress to evaluate.

Should There Be Penalties for Missing the Target?

If one goal of an inflation target is to increase the Fed's accountability to Congress, then a natural question is whether accountability should be buttressed by tangible consequences for bad results. Otherwise, admonitions for missing the target might be ignored. The difficulty with creating penalties is that the Fed's high degree of independence means that many potential penalties could either be toothless or draconian. For example, if a federal agency performed poorly, Congress could reduce or add restrictions to its budget in the following fiscal year. That option is not currently available for the Fed because it is self-financed and has budgetary independence.

One proposed penalty is that a missed target would trigger an automatic report to Congress or a Congressional hearing that would require the Fed to explain why the target was missed and how the situation would be remedied. Another proposed penalty is that the Chairman or Board could be removed if the target were persistently missed or missed by a wide margin. This would be a significant change from current policy, under which governors (including the Chairman) can be removed only for cause.

One argument against explicit penalties is that the Fed could be unfairly punished for events beyond its control, such as an oil price spike. The likelihood of this occurring would depend on the flexibility built into the target and the penalty.

CONCLUSION

Most arguments in favor of an inflation target fall into two categories: improved accountability of monetary policymakers and increased transparency of monetary policy to financial markets. Both are thought to result in better outcomes for the economy. A single mandate or inflation target may constrain the Fed's ability to pursue policies that result in high inflation, but in practice Fed policies over the past two decades have not resulted in high inflation. Nevertheless, past performance does not guarantee similar results in the future. Introducing an inflation target might be a way to "lock in" good policies.

In isolation, a change to a single mandate of price stability is unlikely to lead to a modification in monetary policy decisions since it would leave intact the Fed's independence and discretion to set policy as it sees fit. The dual mandate is only one of many institutional factors that contribute to the Fed's discretion and independence. Neither statute nor tradition formally lay out the consequences of missing the mandated goals; this makes accountability more difficult, but a switch to a single mandate in isolation would not alter that arrangement. An inflation target could potentially have more of an impact on the Fed's discretion, but the extent that its discretion would be constrained would depend on the characteristics of the inflation target, such as what consequences there would be if the target were missed, and whether the inflation target was selected and designed by the Fed or by Congress.

As practiced abroad, countries with a single mandate or inflation target have not ignored changes in unemployment, in part because they may help predict future changes in inflation. While this demonstrates that policymaking under one or both can be more flexible in practice than opponents paint it, it also begs the question of whether dropping maximum employment from the mandate is necessary or desired.

Some of the desire for legislative change comes from discontent with the Fed's recent performance. Therefore this report has analyzed two questions— what are the shortcomings in the Fed's recent performance, and would those shortcomings be affected by a mandate change?

Many of the criticisms of the Fed's performance—its "bailouts" of "too big to fail" firms, lax supervision of the financial system in the run up to the crisis, its passivity during the housing boom's run up of unsuitable mortgage debt—are unrelated to its monetary policy mandate, and involve authority derived from other parts of the Federal Reserve Act. Monetary policy's failure to prevent, and possibly exacerbate, the housing bubble, could argue in support of a mandate change. But because the housing bubble did not lead to high inflation, a single mandate would not likely modify the Fed's behavior in the face of future asset bubbles. A mandate change to require the Fed to explicitly address bubbles or financial stability might be a more effective means to this end. Criticism that the Fed should have done more to prevent the depth and length of the recession implicitly speaks to the "maximum employment" part of the dual mandate, and so a single mandate would be unlikely to result in more aggressive countercyclical policy.

By conventional standards, the Fed's record on price stability in the last two decades is very good—headline inflation has been below 4% since 1991 and core inflation has been below 3% since 1995—but not perfect. It is also not significantly different than major inflation targeting countries. A criticism could be made that the Fed's focus on core inflation has not proven to be the optimal measure for obtaining price stability. But this criticism does not make the case that the Fed has neglected price stability, or that the Fed would be more focused on price stability under a single mandate. Unless Congress is involved in defining price stability (through the type of inflation to be targeted, for example), discretion would still remain with the Fed on what measure to focus on. A similar argument applies to criticisms that the Fed's program of quantitative easing is inconsistent with a price stability mandate—the Fed believes that quantitative easing is necessary to maintain price stability (to avoid deflation), and as long as the Fed has discretion to set its policies, a single mandate would not prevent quantitative easing.

End Notes

[1] P.L. 95-188, 91 Stat. 1387.

[2] Section 2A of the Federal Reserve Act, 12 USC 225a. This language was previously included in House Concurrent Resolution 133 of 1975.

[3] For more information, see CRS Report RL34427, *Financial Turmoil: Federal Reserve Policy Responses*, by Marc Labonte.

[4] Ben Bernanke, Testimony Before the U.S. Senate Committee on Banking, Housing and Urban Affairs, November 15, 2005.

[5] See, for example, Marvin Goodfriend, "Inflation Targeting in the United States?", in Ben Bernanke and Michael Woodford, eds., *The Inflation Targeting Debate* (Chicago: University of Chicago Press, 2004), ch. 8. The Federal Open Market Committee (FOMC), the internal Fed committee that sets monetary policy, already publishes a "longer run" forecast for inflation. Since monetary policy is the primary determinant of inflation in the longer run, this could be seen as the FOMC's implicit inflation target.

[6] This section draws on Ben Bernanke and Michael Woodford, eds., *The Inflation Targeting Debate*, University of Chicago Press, (Chicago: 2004); Ben S. Bernanke et al., *Inflation Targeting* (Princeton: Princeton University Press, 1999); Edwin Truman, *Inflation Targeting*, Institute for International Economics, October 2003; Michael Dueker and Andreas Fischer, "Do Inflation Targeters Outperform Non-Targeters?," *Federal Reserve Bank of St. Louis Review*, September 2006, p. 431; Manfred Neumann and Jurgen von Hagen, "Does Inflation Targeting Matter?", Federal Reserve Bank of St. Louis, *Review*, July 2002, p. 127; Benjamin M. Friedman, Kenneth N. Kuttner, Mark Gertler, James Tobin, "A Price Target for U.S. Monetary Policy? Lessons from the Experience with Money Growth Targets," *Brookings Papers on Economic Activity*, Vol. 1996, No. 1, 1996, p. 77; William McDonough, "A Framework for the Pursuit of Price Stability," *Economic Policy Review*, vol. 3, no. 3 (August 1997), p. 1; Andrew Levin, Fabio Natalucci, Jeremy Piger, "The Macroeconomic Effects of Inflation Targeting," *Federal Reserve Bank of St. Louis Review*, July/Aug. 2004, p. 51; Richard Dennis, "Inflation Targeting Under Commitment and Discretion," *Federal Reserve Bank of San Francisco Economic Review*, 2005, p. 1.

[7] In 2009, the CPI experienced slight deflation, meaning overall prices fell. In this case, inflation was lower than desired. In other words, the one time in recent years it failed to achieve price stability, it was the opposite problem of the one predicted by the economic theory that policymakers are biased toward high inflation.

[8] Similar results are found using other price indices, such as the gross domestic product (GDP) deflator or the PCE (personal consumption expenditures) deflator.

[9] This issue is discussed in depth in the section entitled "Quantitative Easing."
[10] See Michael Dueker and Andreas Fischer, "Do Inflation Targeters Outperform Non-Targeters?", *Federal Reserve Bank of St. Louis, Review*, vol. 88, no. 5, September/October 2006, p. 431.
[11] CRS calculations based on data from the International Monetary Fund, World Economic Outlook database, October 2010.
[12] For more information, see CRS Report RS22705, *Inflation: Core vs. Headline*, by Marc Labonte.
[13] The theory of a natural rate of unemployment posits that the economy will tend toward an equilibrium unemployment rate in the long run. When unemployment is at this "natural rate," inflation will neither rise nor fall. For more information, see CRS Report RL30391, *Inflation and Unemployment: What is the Connection?*, by Brian W. Cashell.
[14] See, for example, Chairman Ben Bernanke, "The Benefits of Price Stability," speech at the Center for Economic Policy Studies, Princeton University, Princeton, New Jersey, February 24, 2006.
[15] "Shoe leather costs" refer to the example that if individuals have to make frequent trips to the bank to prevent inflation from eroding the value of their currency, the leather in their shoes will wear out faster.
[16] Olivier Blanchard, "Remarks at the New School," November 2002, http://econ-www.mit.edu/files/731.
[17] Ben Bernanke and Frederic Mishkin, "Inflation Targeting: A New Framework for Monetary Policy?," *Journal of Economic Perspectives*, vol. 11, no. 2, Spring 1997, p. 97.
[18] A paper from the San Francisco Fed uses simulations to demonstrate that an inflation target where discretionary changes are allowed would have led to monetary policy since the 1980s that is fairly close to the actual policy that the Fed pursued. Richard Dennis, "Inflation Targeting Under Commitment and Discretion," *Federal Reserve Bank of San Francisco Economic Review*, 2005, p. 1.
[19] Kenneth Rogoff, "The Optimal Degree of Commitment to an Intermediate Monetary Target," *Quarterly Journal of Economics*, vol. 100, no. 4, November 1985, p. 1169.
[20] For more information, see CRS Report RL34427, *Financial Turmoil: Federal Reserve Policy Responses*, by Marc Labonte.
[21] In light of its role in the financial crisis, another potential legislative change would be to add lender of last resort duties or a goal of financial stability to the Fed's monetary policy mandate, since these duties are not explicitly enumerated elsewhere in the Federal Reserve Act.
[22] Another argument is that if the Fed had done a better job of regulating mortgage products a housing bubble could have been avoided. This argument is considered in the section below entitled "Lax Supervision of the Financial System and Mortgage Markets."
[23] Chairman Ben S. Bernanke, "Causes of the Recent Financial and Economic Crisis," Testimony before the Financial Crisis Inquiry Commission, Washington, D.C., September 2, 2010.
[24] Chairman Ben S. Bernanke, "Monetary Policy and the Housing Bubble," Speech at the Annual Meeting of the American Economic Association, Atlanta, Georgia, January 3, 2010.
[25] Ben Bernanke, "Asset Price 'Bubbles' and Monetary Policy," Speech before the National Association of Business Economics, New York, NY, October 15, 2002.
[26] The Dodd-Frank Wall Street Reform and Consumer Protection Act (P.L. 111-203) created the Financial Stability Oversight Council (FSOC) to identify risks to financial stability, promote market discipline, and respond to emerging threats to the stability of the U.S. financial system. The Chairman of the Federal Reserve is a member of the FSOC. Including financial

stability in the Fed's mandate could be seen as either complementary or inconsistent with the FSOC.

[27] For more information, see CRS Report R41540, *Quantitative Easing and the Growth in the Federal Reserve's Balance Sheet*, by Marc Labonte.

[28] See, for example, "An Open Letter to Ben Bernanke," November 15, 2010, downloaded at http://economics21.org/ commentary/e21s-open-letter-ben-bernanke.

[29] Federal Open Market Committee, press release, March 18, 2009.

[30] Federal Open Market Committee, press release, November 3, 2010.

[31] For more information, see CRS Report R41073, *Government Interventions in Response to Financial Turmoil*, by Baird Webel and Marc Labonte. While the Fed has sometimes been characterized as "bailing out" Fannie Mae and Freddie Mac, it did not provide any funds directly to those firms. Rather, it purchased securities issued by those firms from other investors on the secondary market as part of its quantitative easing policy.

[32] Chairman Ben S. Bernanke, "Monetary Policy and the Housing Bubble," Speech at the Annual Meeting of the American Economic Association, Atlanta, Georgia, January 3, 2010.

[33] This discussion draws on C.A.E. Goodhart, and Jose Vinals, "Strategy and Tactics of Monetary Policy: Monetary Examples from Europe and the Antipodes" in *Goals, Guidelines, and Constraints Facing Policymakers*, op. cit, pp. 139-187; Guy Debelle and Stanley Fischer, "How Independent Should a Central Bank Be?," ibid, pp. 195-221; and Geoffrey Heenan, Marcel Peter, and Scott Roger, "Implementing Inflation Targeting," International Monetary Fund, working paper 06/278, December 2006; Robert Dittmar, William Gavin, Finn Kydland, "Price-Level Uncertainty and Inflation Targeting," *Federal Reserve Bank of St. Louis Review*, July 1999, pp. 23-33; Richard Dennis, "Bandwidth, Bandlength, and Inflation Targeting: Some Observations," *Reserve Bank of New Zealand Bulletin*, vol. 60, no. 1, 1997; Lars Svensson, *Inflation Forecast Targeting: Implementing and Monitoring Inflation Targets*, European Economic Review, vol. 41, 1997, pp.111-1146; Charles Carlstrom and Timothy Fuerst, "Monetary Policy Rules and Stability: Inflation Targeting versus Price-Level Targeting," *Federal Reserve Bank of Cleveland Economic Commentary*, February 2002; Pierre Siklos, "Inflation-Targeting Design," *Federal Reserve Bank of St. Louis Review*, March/April 1999, p. 47.

[34] The fact that the target can be changed in the future by either the Fed or Congress weakens some of the arguments made in its favor, such as enhanced accountability, transparency, and credibility.

[35] Chairman Alan Greenspan, "Transparency in Monetary Policy," Remarks by At the Federal Reserve Bank of St. Louis, Economic Policy Conference, St. Louis, Missouri (via videoconference), October 11, 2001.

[36] See, for example, George Akerlof, William Dickens, and George Perry, "Near-Rational Wage and Price Setting and the Long-Run Phillips Curve," *Brookings Papers on Economic Activity*, 2000, vol. 1, p. 1.

[37] Olivier Blanchard, Giovanni Dell'Ariccia, and Paolo Mauro, "Rethinking Macroeconomic Policy," International Monetary Fund, *Staff Position Note 10/03*, February 2010.

[38] For more information, see CRS Report RS22705, *Inflation: Core vs. Headline*, by Marc Labonte.

In: The Federal Reserve
Editor: John P. Ranchett

ISBN: 978-1-62100-528-5
© 2011 Nova Science Publishers, Inc.

Chapter 5

INFLATION: CORE VS. HEADLINE[*]

Marc Labonte

SUMMARY

Inflation measures the rate of change in all prices. Maintaining low and stable inflation is one of the primary goals of macroeconomic policy. But how should inflation be measured? Policymakers, particularly at the Federal Reserve, often refer to *core* inflation in their policy decisions. Core inflation is commonly defined as a measure of inflation that omits changes in food and energy prices. Some policymakers prefer to use core inflation to predict future overall inflation because food and energy price volatility makes it difficult to discern trends from the overall inflation rate. A drawback of an over-reliance on core inflation, however, is that an extended period of rapidly rising food or energy prices could cause all other prices to accelerate. A focus on core may cause policymakers to fail to react to such a rise in inflation until it is too late. This scenario may have occurred recently. Many economists are concerned that rapid increases in food and energy prices are now pushing overall inflation to uncomfortably high levels. Furthermore, several studies have failed to find core inflation to be a good forecaster of future inflation, casting doubt on the very rationale for relying on it.

---

[*] This is an edited, reformatted and augmented version of a Congressional Research Service publication, CRS Report for Congress RS22705, dated May 1, 2008.

INTRODUCTION

Inflation, the general rise in the prices of goods and services, is important to policymakers for several reasons.[1] First, rising inflation is unpopular with the public, in part because some households are more adversely affected by inflation than others. Second, high or rising inflation can reduce productivity by distorting price signals, so that it is hard for businesses to tell if prices are changing in relative terms, and by individuals wasting resources in order to maintain the purchasing power of their wealth. Finally, inflation plays a key role in macroeonomic stabilization policy. Changes in inflation often indicate changes in the business cycle — rising inflation is often a sign that the economy is overheating and falling inflation is a sign that the economy is sluggish. The Federal Reserve (Fed) is mandated to keep inflation low and stable, and alters interest rates in order to do so.[2]

In recent years, the Fed has focused attention on the *core* rate of inflation, a measure of inflation that excludes food and energy prices, in explanations of its policy decisions. For example, in July 2007, the third sentence of the 10-sentence Federal Open Market Committee statement summarizing the committee's policy decision read, "Readings on core inflation have improved modestly in recent months." In Fed Chairman Ben Bernanke's July 2007 testimony to Congress, he stated that "Food and energy prices tend to be quite volatile, so that, looking forward, core inflation...may be a better gauge than overall inflation of underlying inflation trends." When core inflation approached 3% in 2006, Chairman Bernanke said that it had "reached a level that, if sustained, would be at or above the upper end of the range that many economists, including myself, would consider consistent with price stability...."[3] This report defines core inflation, reviews recent trends, and analyzes the advantages and drawbacks of using core inflation.

DEFINITION

No official measure of "inflation" exists. Inflation is measured as the percent change in a price index. Several indices track price changes, with each data series measuring something different. The most commonly cited measure of inflation is the percent change in the *consumer price index (CPI)*.[4] This index measures the price of a basket of consumer goods and services that is representative of overall consumer purchases in urban areas. When food and energy prices are omitted from the CPI, the remaining basket is commonly referred to as the *core CPI*. The overall measure of CPI, which includes food and energy, is often referred to as the *headline CPI*. Another common measure of inflation is the percent change in the *GDP (gross domestic product) price deflator*, which is used to transform nominal GDP into real GDP. Since the GDP deflator is based on the prices of all goods and services in the economy, it is a broader measure of inflation than the CPI. A subset of the GDP deflator that is conceptually similar to the CPI, but includes more items and areas, is the *personal consumption expenditures (PCE) price deflator*; for technical reasons, the Fed sometimes prefers this measure to the CPI in their analyses. Core measures of the GDP and PCE deflators are also available.

Conceptually, core inflation could be any measure of inflation that attempts to strip out price volatility, but the most common definition of core strips out only two particularly volatile categories of goods, food and energy. The four most volatile items in the CPI are all food or energy products.[5] The standard deviation of energy prices is estimated to be 12 times higher than overall inflation.[6] Omitting food and energy prices from the CPI is not a trivial modification — food and beverages accounted for 15% of the headline CPI basket, and energy accounted for an additional 9% in 2006.

While excluding food from core inflation has become conventional, it may no longer be warranted. The volatility of food has decreased significantly since the 1970s.[7] Until 2007, the recent divergence between headline and core inflation was driven by energy prices. In 2007, food prices rose rapidly — it is too soon to tell whether this development marks a renewed period of persistent volatility. If food prices are no longer volatile, then policymakers may be losing useful information by omitting them.

RECENT INFLATION TRENDS

In recent years, headline inflation has typically outpaced core inflation, as seen in Figure 1, because of the rapid rise in energy prices. In 2007, headline inflation was also driven up by a 3.9% increase in food prices. The difference between core and headline has not always been trivial — from 2003 to 2006, core inflation was 0.9 percentage points lower than headline. Considering that the Fed judges 2% inflation to be on the low side and 3% inflation on the high side, the definition used in these years would have arguably strongly colored their policy stance. The difference between core and headline inflation over this period was overwhelmingly the result of energy prices, which rose by an average of 12.8% a year as measured by the CPI.

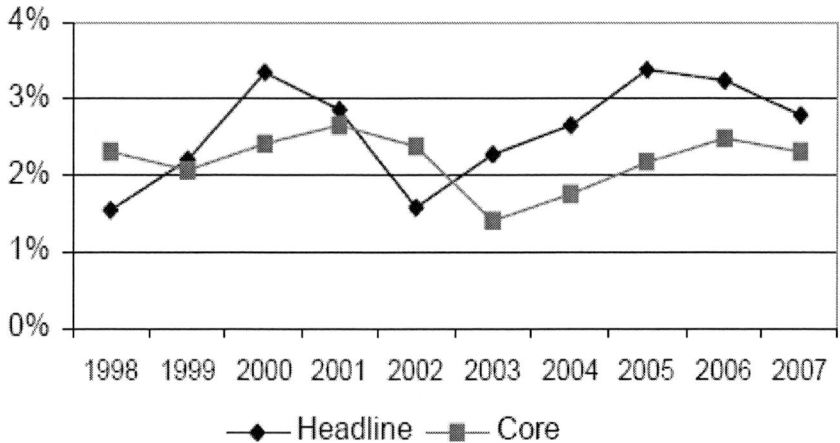

Source: Bureau of Labor Statistics.

Figure 1. Inflation Rate, 1998-2007.

WHEN SHOULD HEADLINE INFLATION BE USED?

When comparing purchasing power over two time periods, headline inflation is the relevant measure. Comparisons over time of wages, wealth, rates of return, government transfers such as Social Security payments, and so on should all use a headline measure of inflation, because all of these concepts depend on a broad measure of inflation. For example, adjusting household income by core inflation would not be useful since food and energy consumption account for about one-quarter of average household expenditures. Similarly, government programs and parts of the tax code that are adjusted for inflation are based on headline inflation. Economic growth is also calculated by first adjusting GDP by headline inflation.

WHEN SHOULD CORE INFLATION BE USED?

Core inflation is used by policymakers for the reason offered by Chairman Bernanke in the introduction — policymakers are most concerned about the future path of inflation, and current core inflation data may give better information than current headline data about future headline inflation. Headline inflation often does not have good predictive power over short-time periods because food and energy prices are so volatile. For example, the monthly headline inflation rate varied between -6.3% and 7.5% in 2006 at annualized rates, whereas the core rate varied between 1.2% and 3.6%.[8] Policymakers are concerned with future inflation because of lags between a change in policy and its effect on the economy. In essence, it is already too late for policy to influence current inflation, a policy change today can only affect future inflation.

Theoretically, short-term changes in inflation can be caused by the supply-side or demand-side of the economy. When rising inflation is demand-driven, it means that spending is growing too quickly in the overall economy, and production cannot keep pace. This phenomenon is captured in the famous saying "too much money chasing too few goods." The Fed's task is to counteract this by raising interest rates in order to reduce the growth rate of interest-sensitive spending. Likewise, if spending is rising too slowly, inflation will fall, which the Fed can counteract by reducing interest rates.

In the short run, the overall inflation rate can also be affected by sharp price changes of individual goods caused by supply shocks. For example, bad weather can drive up food prices or a reduction in the oil supply can drive up energy prices. Since these supply shocks are temporary, they should not have any lasting effect on inflation (holding aggregate spending constant), in which case they can be ignored by policymakers. In the long run, price shocks on the supply side should cancel each other out (since, across all goods, there will be an equal number of positive and negative surprises), and average inflation should be completely demand driven.

Ideally, policymakers would like to be able to identify whether any change in inflation was demand-driven or supply-driven. Unfortunately, there is no straightforward way to do this, so they have commonly used core inflation as a proxy for demand-driven inflation, reasoning that food and energy are two sectors of the economy that are most susceptible to supply shocks. Furthermore, policymakers are particularly concerned with inflationary expectations, and a rising core rate may be a better sign than rising headline that inflationary expectations have risen.

Relying on core inflation for policymaking has its drawbacks, however. There is no inherent reason that changes in food and energy prices cannot be caused by changes in aggregate demand. For example, rapid spending growth could push up energy prices if supply does not rise in response. In fact, an argument has been made that a change in aggregate demand would first show up in price changes of goods that have flexible pricing, such as commodities that are traded on financial markets where prices change continually to clear the market.[9] Both energy and basic foodstuffs are traded on financial markets, although the CPI measures final food and energy products, not basic commodities.

Furthermore, a rise in the price of any one good need not lead to a change in inflation if the prices of other goods fall to offset it. Technically, if a rise in one price leads to a rise in overall inflation, it must be because of some accommodation on the Fed's part (because it did not raise interest rates enough to induce other prices to fall). Most economists believe that some accommodation to relative price changes is desirable because it reduces the volatility of economic growth, whereas zero accommodation could lead to needless disruptions in economic activity. For example, Fed Governor Frederic Mishkin used the Fed's macro model of the U.S. economy to show that when the Fed reacts to changes in headline inflation instead of core inflation, future inflation will be slightly less volatile, but unemployment will be significantly more volatile.[10] But if the Fed accommodates a rise in the price of one good too much, then the price of all goods could start rising. In other words, a rise in headline inflation could feed through to higher core inflation. This scenario occurred in the 1970s where rising energy prices resulted in a rise in total inflation.

In scenarios like this one, a focus on core inflation could forestall a needed policy change until it is too late. Indeed, a case can be made today that more of a focus on headline inflation would have avoided the persistent upward trend in core inflation that has occurred from 2003 to 2007 and brought core inflation above the Fed's self-defined "comfort zone." The weakness with the focus on core inflation is that when energy prices rise continually for a period of several years, they no longer represent random price fluctuations that offer no useful information about future inflation. As a result, too much monetary policy accommodation may have taken place recently, causing the economy to overheat. Future events will reveal if this is the case, or if the rise in core inflation can be painlessly reversed without a recession.

In the end, the question of what measure of inflation is best for policymaking is an empirical one. One study found that "no core measure does an outstanding job forecasting [headline] CPI inflation...we find no strong evidence to suggest that a selected core measure will be able to retain its usefulness as a tool to forecast inflation for any given period..."[11] Another study did not find a statistically significant relationship between core inflation and future headline inflation, although the relationship becomes significant when limited to a more recent time period.[12] Two other studies found that headline inflation is a better predictor of future headline inflation than core inflation.[13] An explanation for this finding is that during the past 10 years, changes in core inflation have tended to lag behind changes in headline inflation as illustrated in Figure 1. One study found that a core measure that excludes only energy was a better predictor of future inflation from 1983 to 2001 than a measure excluding food and energy. In fact, that study found food prices to be a better predictor of future inflation than any other measure, including core inflation.[14] Some studies suggest that there may be more sophisticated measurements that are better gauges of underlying inflationary pressures than the standard definition of core inflation.[15] Core inflation has the advantage from a policy perspective, however, of being transparent, whereas the more sophisticated measurements could be hard for the public to understand and open to accusations of data mining or manipulation. While this advantage may make core inflation a useful tool for communicating Fed policy to the public, the empirical evidence suggests it to be, by itself, an inadequate tool for policymaking.

End Notes

[1] For more information, see CRS Report RL30344, *Inflation: Causes, Costs, and Current Status*, by Marc Labonte and Gail Makinen.
[2] For more information, see CRS Report RL30354, *Monetary Policy and the Federal Reserve*, by Marc Labonte and Gail Makinen.
[3] Chairman Ben S. Bernanke, "Panel Discussion: Comments on the Outlook for the U.S. Economy and Monetary Policy," at the International Monetary Conference, Washington, DC, June 5, 2006.
[4] For more information, see CRS Report RL30074, *The Consumer Price Index: A Brief Overview*, by Brian W. Cashell.
[5] Todd Clark, "Comparing Measures of Core Inflation," Federal Reserve Bank of Kansas City, *Economic Review*, 2002:2, p. 5. The four most volatile items are fuel oil, motor fuel, meats and dairy products, and fruits and vegetables.
[6] Seamus Smyth, "Why Care About Core?," Goldman Sachs, *U.S. Daily Financial Market Comment*, September 7, 2006.
[7] William Gavin and Rachel Mandal, "Predicting Inflation: Food for Thought," Federal Reserve Bank of St. Louis, *Regional Economist*, January 2002.
[8] Of course, volatility is lower over longer time horizons, so policymakers also judge inflationary pressures by looking at, say, the 12-month change in inflation rather than the one-month change. In 2006, the 12-month change in headline inflation varied between 1.3% to 4.3%, and 12-month core inflation varied between 2.1% and 2.9%.
[9] Brian Motley, "Should Monetary Policy Focus on Core Inflation?," Federal Reserve Bank of San Francisco, *Economic Letter*, no. 97-11, April 1997.

[10] Frederic Mishkin, "Headline versus Core Inflation in the Conduct of Monetary Policy," speech at the Business Cycles, International Transmission and Macroeconomic Policies Conference, Montreal, Canada, October 20, 2007.

[11] Robert Rich and Charles Steindel, "A Review of Core Inflation and an Evaluation of Its Measures," Federal Reserve Bank of New York, staff report no. 236, December 2005. The study examines the forecasting power of inflation less food and energy, as well as alternative definitions of core inflation that have been proposed by others.

[12] Todd Clark, "Comparing Measures of Core Inflation," Federal Reserve Bank of Kansas City, *Economic Review*, 2002:2, p. 5.

[13] Michael Bryan and Stephen Cecchetti, "Measuring Core Inflation," in N. Gregory Mankiw, ed., *Monetary Policy* (Chicago: University of Chicago Press, 1994), p. 195; and Julie Smith, "Weighted Median Inflation: Is This Core Inflation?," *Journal of Money, Credit, and Banking*, April 2004, vol. 36, no. 2, p. 253. Both studies compared the forecasting ability of many measures of inflation, and concluded that a weighted median measure of inflation performed best.

[14] William Gavin and Rachel Mandal, "Predicting Inflation: Food for Thought," Federal Reserve Bank of St. Louis, *Regional Economist*, January 2002.

[15] Economists have tried to find the best measure of core inflation according to different criteria. See Timothy Cogley, "A Simple Adaptive Measure of Core Inflation," *Journal of Money, Credit and Banking*, vol. 34, no. 1, February 2002, pp. 94-113; Danny Quah; Shaun P. Vahey, "Measuring Core Inflation," *The Economic Journal*, vol. 105, no. 432, September 1995, pp. 1130-1144; Michael Bryan and Stephen Cecchetti, "Measuring Core Inflation," in N. Gregory Mankiw, ed., *Monetary Policy*, (Chicago: University of Chicago Press, 1994), p. 195; Todd Clark, "Comparing Measures of Core Inflation," Federal Reserve Bank of Kansas City, *Economic Review*, 2002:2, p. 5.

In: The Federal Reserve
Editor: John P. Ranchett

ISBN: 978-1-62100-528-5
© 2011 Nova Science Publishers, Inc.

Chapter 6

QUANTITATIVE EASING AND THE GROWTH IN THE FEDERAL RESERVE'S BALANCE SHEET[*]

Marc Labonte

SUMMARY

On November 3, 2010, the Federal Reserve (Fed) announced that it would purchase an additional $600 billion of Treasury securities, an action that has popularly been dubbed quantitative easing or "QE2." This announcement followed purchases since March 2009 of $300 billion of Treasury securities, $175 billion of agency debt, and $1.25 trillion of agency mortgage-backed securities (MBS). (The agency debt and MBS were primarily issued by Fannie Mae and Freddie Mac.) This report defines quantitative easing as actions to further stimulate the economy through growth in the Fed's balance sheet once the federal funds rate has reached the "zero bound."

In its announcement of QE2, the Fed justified its decision by citing the "disappointingly slow" progress to date toward achieving its statutory mandate of maximum employment and stable prices. By contrast, critics believe that unconventional monetary actions such as QE2 could be destabilizing and ultimately result in high inflation.

---

[*] This is an edited, reformatted and augmented version of a Congressional Research Service publication, CRS Report for Congress R41540, from www.crs.gov, dated December 21, 2010.

There are several ways that quantitative easing can affect the economy. It would be expected to reduce yields on the securities being purchased, and this could have a cascading downward effect on private yields that could stimulate investment spending. Like any monetary stimulus, it could put downward pressure on the dollar, which would stimulate exports and U.S. production of import-competing goods. The initial quantitative easing following the 2008 crisis helped restore liquidity to the financial system, although this channel is arguably not as important now that liquidity has generally been restored. Finally, the direct effect of quantitative easing to date has been to increase bank reserves by over $1 trillion. If banks choose to lend these reserves, it would stimulate economic activity and increase the money supply. But lending has fallen in the past year, and there have been only relatively modest increases in the overall money supply.

Nevertheless, the increase in bank reserves could eventually result in large increases in the overall money supply, which could arguably make it difficult for the Fed to meet its statutory mandate to keep inflation low and stable. The Fed has explored different methods of unwinding quantitative easing if inflationary pressures rose, which have been referred to as the "exit strategy." One method would be to directly reverse quantitative easing by selling some or all of the additional securities that the Fed has purchased, which would automatically withdraw reserves from the banking system. A drawback to this approach is that large sales of securities would probably involve selling its mortgage-related securities, and this could be destabilizing to a housing market that is still sluggish. Another method would be to raise the interest rate that the Fed has been paying to banks on reserves since 2008 to a level high enough that it would give banks an incentive to keep the funds parked at the Fed rather than lending them out. This approach is largely untested, however, and the associated expenditure could become large relative to the Fed's overall profits at historically normal levels of interest rates.

Since the Fed remits most of its profits to the Treasury, where these are added to general revenues, both quantitative easing and its unwinding have implications for the federal budget deficit. Since quantitative easing increases the amount of income-earning securities held by the Fed, it would be expected to increase its profits and reduce the federal budget deficit. Indeed, profits increased from $38.8 billion in 2008 to $52.4 billion in 2009. Similarly, unwinding QE would be expected to reduce the Fed's profits. Some critics have argued that the Fed is monetizing the budget deficit through QE2. The Fed is legally prohibited from purchasing federal debt directly from the Treasury, but Fed purchases of Treasury securities on the open market have a similar effect on the budget deficit as if those purchases were made directly.

INTRODUCTION

On November 3, 2010, the Federal Reserve (Fed) announced that it would purchase an additional $600 billion of Treasury securities, an action that has popularly been dubbed quantitative easing or "QE2."[1] This announcement followed purchases of $300 billion of Treasury securities, $175 billion of agency debt, and $1.25 trillion of agency mortgage-backed securities (MBS) since March 2009.[2] While there may not be a universally accepted definition of quantitative easing, this report defines quantitative easing as actions to further stimulate the economy through growth in the Fed's balance sheet once the federal funds rate has reached the "zero bound." By this definition, quantitative easing has not been tried in the United States before, although it was implemented in Japan from 2001 to 2006.[3]

Congress has given the Fed a statutory mandate to "promote effectively the goals of maximum employment, stable prices, and moderate long-term interest rates,"[4] and the Fed has made the case that quantitative easing can help it to fulfill its mandate. In its announcement of QE2, the Fed explained its decision by citing "disappointingly slow" progress toward achieving a reduction in unemployment and stable inflation, which has been falling.[5] By contrast, critics argue that unconventional monetary actions such as QE2 could be destabilizing and ultimately result in high inflation. For example, an open letter from a group of economists to Fed Chairman Ben Bernanke on November 15 stated, "The planned asset purchases risk currency debasement and inflation, and we do not think they will achieve the Fed's objective of promoting employment."[6]

This report discusses the Fed's actions to stimulate the economy through quantitative easing from September 2008 to the announcement of a further round of quantitative easing in November 2010 (popularly referred to as QE2). This report evaluates arguments for and against QE2 in the context of the current economic outlook, the intended and estimated economic effects of quantitative easing, as well as future concerns regarding the "exit strategy" for eventually returning to a more conventional monetary policy. It also addresses concerns about whether the Fed is monetizing the federal debt and what effects QE2 might have on the federal budget deficit.

OVERVIEW OF FEDERAL RESERVE ACTIONS SINCE 2007

Normally, monetary policy is conducted by setting a target for the federal funds rate, the overnight inter-bank lending rate. To keep the actual federal funds rate (determined by the supply and demand for bank reserves) near the target, the Fed regularly buys and sells Treasury securities. Before 2007, the Fed's balance sheet consisted overwhelmingly of Treasury securities, with a very modest growth in the portfolio over time. While the Fed has always lent to banks at its discount window, the amount of loans outstanding has typically been less than $1 billion. It had not lent to non-banks since the 1930s. Beginning in December 2007, the Fed undertook a series of unprecedented policy steps that fundamentally departed from traditional policy.

Beginning in 2007, the Fed reduced its target for the federal funds rate in a series of steps to a range of 0% to 0.25% on December 16, 2008. Since the federal funds rate cannot be reduced below zero, the Fed could deliver no additional stimulus through conventional policy. Deeming conventional policy to be insufficient given the state of the economy in September 2008, the Fed turned to quantitative easing even before its federal funds target reached to zero, as will be discussed below.

Phase One: Direct Lending and Initial Balance Sheet Growth

From December 2007 to October 2008, the Fed introduced a series of emergency lending facilities for banks and non-bank financial firms and markets to restore liquidity to the financial system.[7] Lending under these facilities is reported as assets on the Fed's balance sheet. To prevent these facilities from leading to an expansion in the size of the Fed's overall balance sheet and the money supply, the Fed "sterilized" (offset) the effects of the facilities on its balance sheet until September 2008 by selling a cumulative $315 billion of its Treasury securities, as seen in Figure 1.

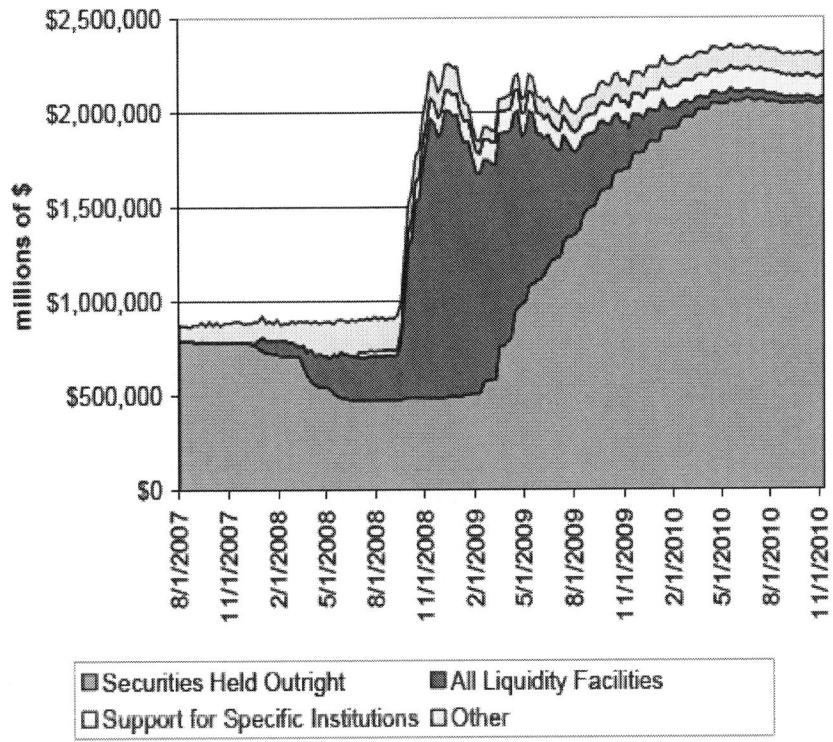

Source: Federal Reserve.

Figure 1. Assets on the Federal Reserve's Balance Sheet, 2007-2010.

When the financial crisis dramatically worsened in September 2008, private liquidity became scarce, causing the Fed's support to the financial system to increase significantly. The increase in support made it impractical for the Fed—if it had desired—to continue sterilizing these loans through asset sales. Instead, the Fed allowed its balance sheet to grow as lending to the financial system increased. Between September and November 2008, the Fed's balance sheet more than doubled in size, increasing from under $1 trillion to over $2 trillion. Over the same period, support offered through liquidity facilities and for specific institutions (including the private security holdings of the Fed's Maiden Lane facilities) increased from about $260 billion to $1.4 trillion.[8]

Since there was no longer any sterilization of its lending, the increase in assets on the Fed's balance sheet was now matched by an increase in its liabilities. The Fed's three main liabilities are Federal Reserve notes, bank reserves held at the Fed, and Treasury deposits held at the Fed— all three items are, in effect, "IOUs" from the Fed to the bearer. As the Fed's assets increased, the primary liability to increase was bank reserves, as seen in Figure 2. The sum of outstanding Federal Reserve notes and bank reserves form the "monetary base," or the portion of the money supply controlled by the Fed.

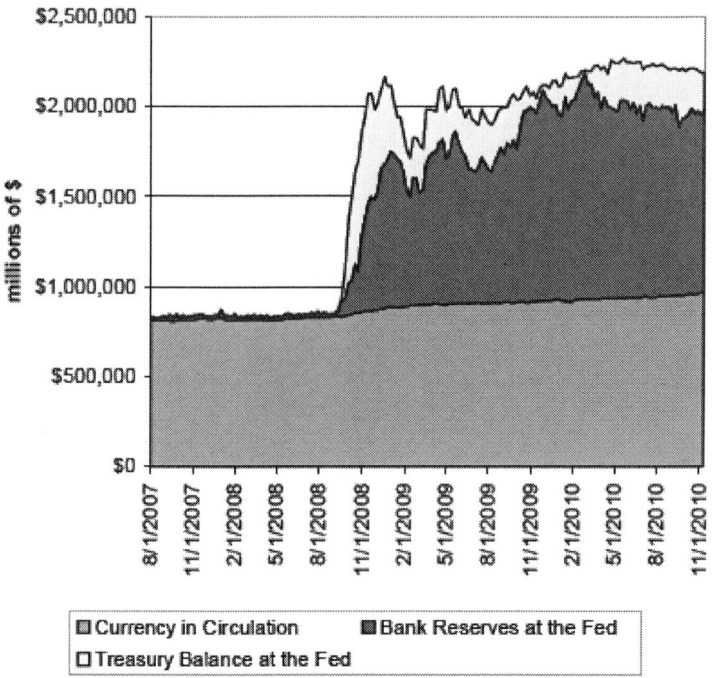

Source: Federal Reserve.

Figure 2. Selected Liabilities on the Fed's Balance Sheet, 2007-2010.

The increase in bank reserves can be seen as the inevitable outcome of the increase in assets held by the Fed. These reserves, in effect, finance the Fed's asset purchases and loan programs. In the case of lending facilities, reserves increase because the loan amounts are credited to the recipient's reserve account at the Fed. In the case of asset purchases, the funds to finance the purchase are credited to the seller's reserve account at the Fed, or if the seller is not a member of the Federal Reserve system, the funds eventually lead to an increase in a member bank's reserves as the proceeds get deposited into the banking system.

Phase Two: Large Scale Asset Purchases from Spring 2009 to Spring 2010

By the beginning of 2009, demand for loans from the Fed was falling as financial conditions normalized. Had the Fed done nothing to offset the fall in lending, the balance sheet would have shrunk by a commensurate amount, and the stimulus that it had added to the economy would have been withdrawn. The Fed judged that the economy, which remained in a recession at that point, still needed this stimulus. On March 18, 2009, the Fed announced a commitment to purchase $300 billion of Treasury securities, $200 billion of agency debt (later revised to $175 billion), and $1.25 trillion of agency mortgage-backed securities.[9]

Since then, the Fed's direct lending has continued to gradually decline, while the Fed's holdings of Treasury and agency securities have steadily increased, as seen in Figure 1. Most emergency lending facilities were allowed to expire in February 2010; by that point emergency lending had fallen to about $200 billion overall, and consisted mostly of the Term Asset-Backed Securities

Loan Facility, Maiden Lane holdings, and assistance to the American International Group (AIG). The Fed's planned purchases of Treasury securities were completed by the fall of 2009 and planned agency purchases were completed by the spring of 2010. By this point, the recession had officially ended. The net result of the Fed's actions in phase two was to keep the overall size of the balance sheet relatively constant.

Once the phase two purchases were completed, the Fed faced a decision on what to do about its maturing short-term assets. If the Fed did not replace securities as they matured, its balance sheet would gradually decline at a pace of about $100 billion to $200 billion per year, according to Chairman Bernanke.[10] To prevent that, the Fed announced on August 10, 2010, that it would replace maturing securities (whether they be Treasury, agency, or mortgage-backed securities) with Treasury security purchases.[11]

Phase Three: Quantitative Easing 2 (November 2010)

Dissatisfied with the slow pace of the economic expansion, the Fed announced on November 3, 2010 that it would further increase the size of its balance sheet by purchasing an additional $600 billion of Treasury securities at a pace of about $75 billion per month, and continue the practice of replacing maturing securities with Treasury security purchases. The Fed's announced intention is to purchase securities with maturity lengths primarily between 2 1/2 to 10 years.[12]

THE ECONOMIC CONTEXT OF QE2

Congress has given the Fed a statutory mandate to pursue stable prices and maximum employment.[13] In the Fed's view, further stimulus is required to meet both goals—unemployment is too high and price inflation is uncomfortably close to zero and falling. In its November 3, 2010, announcement, the Fed gave the following reason for pursuing QE2:

> Currently, the unemployment rate is elevated, and measures of underlying inflation are somewhat low, relative to levels that the Committee judges to be consistent, over the longer run, with its [statutory] dual mandate. Although the Committee anticipates a gradual return to higher levels of resource utilization in a context of price stability, progress toward its objectives has been disappointingly slow.
> To promote a stronger pace of economic recovery and to help ensure that inflation, over time, is at levels consistent with its mandate, the Committee decided today to expand its holdings of securities.[14]

The National Bureau of Economic Research (NBER) dated the end of the recent recession as June 2009. Beginning in the third quarter of 2009, gross domestic product rose, and it has grown modestly each quarter since then. Unemployment has fallen from a high of 10.1% in October 2009 to 9.8% in November 2010. Since World War II, the only other period when unemployment was above 9.5% was from 1982 to 1983. Most economic forecasters are predicting that the economy will continue to grow at a similar pace through 2011, and that unemployment will continue to top 9% through the end of 2011.[15]

There are two downside risks to the consensus view on the economic outlook that can be considered unlikely but not implausible. There is a fear the economy will experience "double dip" recessions, meaning a return to economic contraction in the near term. By historical standards double dips are rare—in the 20th century, there were two cases where the economy emerged from a recession, only to be quickly followed by another recession (beginning in 1920 and 1981).[16] In 1981, a large tightening of monetary policy is seen as playing a key role in the economy's return to recession, unlike today. The usual pattern is that once the expansion takes root (as the NBER has determined has happened), it continues for some time. For the expansion to be knocked off course and the economy to return to recession, some new "shock" to the economy would likely be needed, such as economic crisis throughout Europe, perhaps following a sovereign default. By their nature, shocks are hard to foresee, but large shocks are relatively infrequent.

Another scenario is that the economy does not re-enter recession, but nor does it experience its usual steady return to full employment and normal growth rates. Instead, it experiences long-term stagnation, sometimes referred to as a deflationary or liquidity trap, where overall spending does not grow quickly enough to reduce significantly the slack in the economy.[17] Evidence in favor of this scenario is the weakness of the expansion to date and the fact that the economy may still be suffering from a debt overhang, where businesses and consumers are "deleveraging" (increasing saving, and in some cases selling assets, to reduce debt).

While the United States has not experienced such stagnation in the post-World War II period, Japan's experience since its equity and real estate bubbles burst in the early 1990s illustrates that this scenario is possible in a modern economy. From 1980 to 1991, GDP growth in Japan averaged 3.8%. Since 1991, GDP growth has never exceeded 2.9% in a year, and from 1992 to 2003, GDP growth was below 2% in all but two years. From a low starting point, Japan's unemployment rate rose each year from 1991 to 2002. From 1995 to 2009, Japan experienced 10 years of deflation (falling prices) and low inflation in the other years, which indicates that Japan's low growth was in part due to inadequate aggregate demand. Although the central bank lowered overnight interest rates to low nominal levels and budget deficits were large (5.6% of GDP on average from 1993 to 2009), Japan was not able to break out of its deflationary trap. The Bank of Japan eventually tried quantitative easing in 2001, but on a smaller scale than the Fed (its balance sheet increased by about 70% overall).[18] Further, some economists believe that Japan's deflationary trap was prolonged by sporadic attempts by the government to withdraw fiscal and monetary stimulus prematurely. Balance sheet growth was withdrawn in 2006 when inflation was still below 1% and economic growth was about 2%; prices and output began shrinking again following the 2008 financial crisis. Many economists believe it was prolonged by Japan's failure to address problems in its financial system following its financial crash.

As discussed below, one often-mentioned concern is that QE2 will lead to high inflation. While this is possible, the larger QE1 has not resulted in any increase in inflation in any of the major indices so far. On the contrary, inflation has been below average and falling. For example, in the last 12 months, the consumer price index has risen by 1.2% and the core consumer price index has risen by 0.6%. For most of 2009, the consumer price index fell compared to the previous 12 months, meaning the economy experienced deflation. Inflationary expectations have also remained low so far, despite the attention that QE2 has brought to the issue.

Based on the consensus forecast, QE2 has been justified on the grounds that the pace of the economy's return to full employment is intolerably slow and inflation has persistently been lower than the Fed's "comfort zone."[19] Alternatively, QE2 could be opposed on the grounds that it is not needed because the economic recovery is firmly rooted. In that view, if the only benefit of QE2 is to return to full employment a little quicker, it is better not to risk fueling inflationary pressures or undermining the Fed's credibility, since both would be costly to reverse in the future. Both of the downside risks to the forecast—a double dip recession or a deflationary trap—argue more strongly in favor of pursuing QE2. If these scenarios materialized, there would arguably be little harm in QE2 as announced, and it might be criticized for being insufficient to ward them off. It is unclear whether opponents of QE2 believe that the projected pace of recovery is sufficient, or if they believe that unconventional monetary policy is inappropriate even if economic conditions are still sluggish once the federal funds rate has reached the zero bound.

While both of the downside scenarios are seen as unlikely, there appear to be even fewer forecasters who are predicting that the economy will grow so much more quickly than the consensus forecast that inflationary pressures will become a problem in the short run, or that inflationary expectations will become ungrounded in the short run.[20] Therefore, arguments against QE2 on inflationary grounds are more persuasive in the context of long term rather than imminent problems with inflation. If the stimulus from QE2 could be effectively unwound in time, then these long-run fears need never be realized. Thus, whether or not QE2 poses long-term risks to price stability revolve around whether the Fed has a viable exit strategy. This is discussed below in the section entitled "Exit Strategy."

ECONOMIC EFFECTS OF QUANTITATIVE EASING

Some forecasters have tried to estimate how much quantitative easing will affect interest rates and economic growth. Former Fed vice chairman Donald Kohn, while acknowledging great uncertainties, estimated that QE1 could increase nominal GDP by as much as $1 trillion over the next several years relative to a baseline forecast.[21] Goldman Sachs estimated that the Fed's previous actions were equivalent to an easing in financial conditions of 1.6 percentage points and predicts that QE2 had an effect equivalent to a 0.8 percentage point easing in financial conditions, which could boost GDP growth by 0.5 percentage points over the next year.[22] Given that this was the estimated effect that occurred between August (when the Fed first began hinting at QE2) and November 4 (when it was officially announced), it remains to be seen whether this estimate will prove accurate and whether the effect will be long lasting. The forecasting firm Macroeconomic Advisors predicts that QE2 – which they believe will be expanded in the future – would raise GDP growth by 0.3 percentage points next year.[23] Given there is no previous experience with quantitative easing in the United States, these estimates are highly speculative. Uncertainty about the effectiveness of quantitative easing makes it difficult to accurately estimate the magnitude of asset purchases needed to achieve the intended stimulus. Furthermore, monetary policy's effect on the economy is gradual, so QE2's full effects will take time and QE1's effects may not yet have completely materialized.

Unless there has been a fundamental change in the economic environment, the effects of QE2 could be expected to be similar to those of QE1, but proportionately smaller. This section discusses four transmission channels through which quantitative easing could affect the economy, and reviews data and research that have attempted to estimate how much QE1 affected the economy.

Liquidity Channel

The initial aim of QE1, the Fed's balance sheet expansion, was to restore liquidity to the financial system, which in late 2008 was highly dysfunctional. Virtually all short-term markets on which financial firms heavily rely on a regular basis were frozen at that time, including interbank lending markets, commercial paper markets, and repurchase agreement ("repo") markets. Most economists believe the Fed's emergency facilities were highly successful in restoring liquidity, although some argue that the system could have healed itself. At this point, financial conditions have normalized enough that further increasing financial market liquidity is arguably not an important goal of QE2.

One view is that emergency lending was necessary to fulfill the Fed's lender of last resort role, but that the Fed's balance sheet should have been allowed to shrink when demand for emergency programs receded, allowing liquidity to be allocated by private markets as soon as it was sufficiently available again. QE1 has left a lasting imprint on the interbank lending market, where large excess reserve holdings have reduced the demand for private interbank borrowing. If one takes that position, however, there remains the dilemma of what role monetary policy should play if the economy is not returning to full employment when policy interest rates are at the zero bound.

Money Multiplier/Bank Lending Channel

Any increase in the asset side of the Fed's balance sheet is matched by an increase in the liability side of the balance sheet. The initial result of an increase in the Fed's asset holdings, whether they be purchases of securities or direct lending, is an increase in bank reserves. In normal times, banks would be expected to lend out those reserves, and this would stimulate overall spending in the economy. While one cannot directly track what banks have done with these reserves, bank lending has fallen 0.3% over the last year, so overall it appears that banks have been mainly content to hold these reserves at the Fed, short circuiting this channel as an effective stimulus.[24] Banks could choose to maintain these reserves instead of lending them for a number of reasons— to increase their liquidity, to reduce the riskiness of their overall portfolio, because they do not believe the profitable lending opportunities exist, because demand for loans by borrowers has declined, or because they face capital constraints that inhibit their ability to increase lending. For those who believe that quantitative easing is "pushing on a string," the approximately $1 trillion increase in excess bank reserves over the past two years is compelling evidence to make that case.

The bank lending channel, if too successful, would also lead to a rapid increase in the overall money supply through the "money multiplier" effect, which in normal times would lead to a rapid increase in inflationary pressures.[25] The increase in the Fed's balance sheet has been matched virtually one-to-one by an increase in that portion of the money supply which is controlled by the Fed, called the monetary base. Normally, banks would lend out money they received from the Fed, and through a process referred to by economists as the "money multiplier," every $1 increase in the monetary base would lead to a much larger increase in the overall money supply. But if banks hold the money received from the Fed in bank reserves instead of lending it out, the money multiplier process will not occur, so the growth in the overall money supply will be smaller. Data from the Fed show that almost all of the increase in reserves has been through reserves in excess of what regulators require, which is consistent with banks holding most of the increase in reserves instead of lending them out. Thus, the unprecedented doubling of the monetary base in a year beginning in August 2008 has resulted in relatively modest increases in the overall money supply, shown in Figure 3 as M1 and M2. In fact, the monetary base is now larger than M1, which has never happened in the past 50 years for which data are available, and all measures of inflation are currently extremely low, as was discussed above.[26]

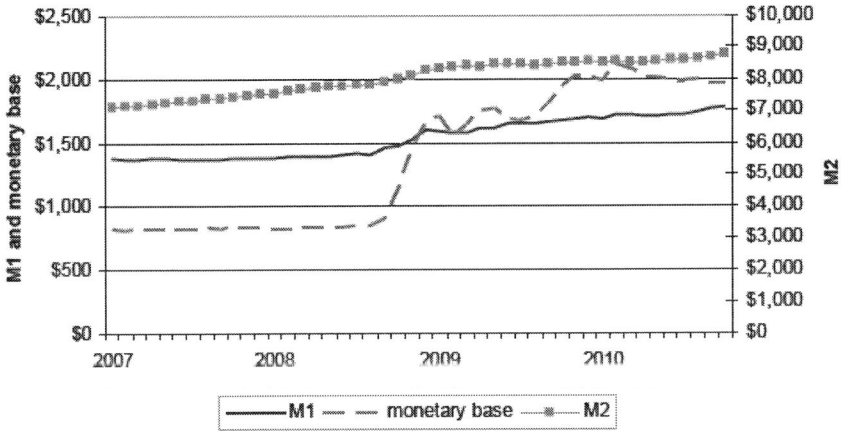

Source: Federal Reserve.

Figure 3. Measures of the Money Supply, 2007-2010; Billions of dollars.

Based on the experience to date, QE2 can also be expected to lead to an increase in bank reserves similar in size to the amount of assets being purchased. It remains to be seen whether QE2 will have a larger effect on banking lending and broader measures of the money supply than QE1 did.

Asset Yield/Portfolio Rebalancing Channel

Even if the money multiplier channel has become blocked by the growth in excess bank reserves, quantitative easing may still stimulate the economy through other channels. The Fed has stressed the asset yield channel in its explanations of the benefits of quantitative easing.[27] Traditional monetary stimulus is limited to altering short-term rates (the federal funds rate). But long-term investment projects are likely to be financed at longer-term rates. By buying longer-term securities, quantitative easing could lead to a flattening of the yield curve (i.e., pushing down long interest rates relative to short rates). Before the crisis, the Fed held about 50% of its Treasury securities with a remaining maturity date of less than a year and 20% with a maturity date of five years or more. Under QE2, the Fed plans to buy no Treasury securities with a maturity of less than a year and over 50% with a maturity of 5 1/2 years or more. A Federal Reserve Bank of San Francisco study estimates that QE1 reduced long-term interest rates by 0.5 to 0.75 percentage points, and cites evidence that long-term rates are more stimulative than equivalent reductions in short-term rates.[28]

The expected direct effect of asset purchases would be to reduce the yields on the assets being purchased. In the case of Treasury securities, lower Treasury yields would have little direct effect on the economy. But if lower Treasury yields cascade through to a broader reduction in interest rates on private securities, this would normally stimulate business investment spending on plant and equipment. How stimulative this "portfolio rebalancing" channel would be depends on how much private yields fall when Treasury yields fall, how sensitive firms are to interest rate changes and, in the present context, how many firms have access to credit markets.[29]

Most research on QE1 found that it had modest but tangible effects on broader interest rates.[30] Its concentration on purchasing mortgage-related assets suggests that it had the largest effects on mortgage rates. As shown in Figure 4, a simple comparison of yields before and after QE1 does not show any obvious impact from QE1—yields on Treasury securities and mortgage rates were relatively flat for about a year after QE1 was implemented, with no downward trend for Treasury or mortgage rates beginning until the spring of 2010, after QE1 was completed. Yields on BAArated corporate bonds did fall after QE1, but the downward trend predated QE1. Unfortunately, the improvement in economic conditions and normalization of financial conditions was probably pushing Treasury yields up and private yields down at the same time, so more sophisticated methods are needed to attempt to disentangle the effects of QE1. Furthermore, conventional mortgage rates were influenced by the government's decision to take the GSEs into conservatorship in September 2008. Some commentators have attributed the decline in yields since August 2010 to QE2 although it has not started yet, on the grounds that investors began anticipating QE2 by that point (several announcements by Fed officials hinted that the Fed was considering QE2 beginning in August) and have already adjusted expectations to take it into account.[31]

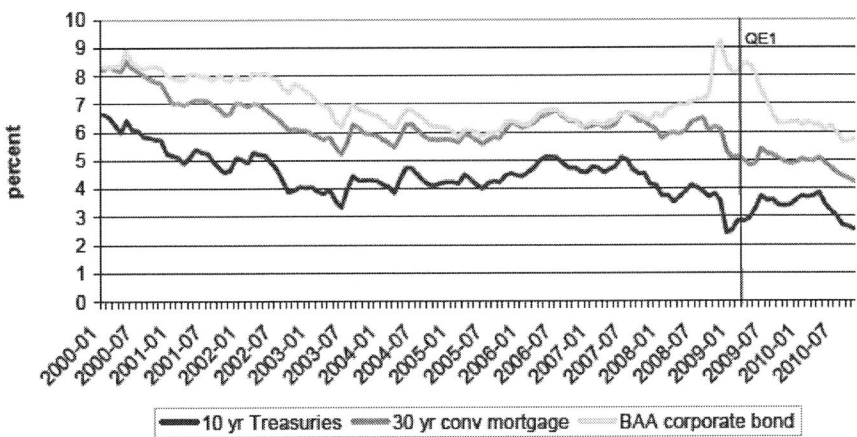

Source: Federal Reserve.

Figure 4. Selected Yields Before and After QE1, 2000-2010.

Research by the New York Fed concludes that QE1 was effective in lowering interest rates based on the immediate response of rates to official announcements about the purchases, although this research could be questioned on the grounds that the rate reductions must be long-lasting to be stimulative, and for some of the maturities in question, interest rates over the entire period rose, on balance.[32] Interpreting the overall effect on interest rates during the life of the asset purchase program is complicated by the fact that other changes in economic conditions also influence interest rates. The authors also use time-series evidence to estimate that the purchase program reduced the yield on ten-year securities relative to short-term securities by 0.38 to 0.82 percentage points. A similar study of the Treasury securities purchased in QE1 found that it reduced Treasury yields by about 0.5 percentage points across the yield curve, with larger effects for long-term securities.[33]

Evidence that QE1 pushed down mortgage rates could potentially suffer from omitted variable bias—namely, the change in the risk-premium associated with MBS over the period in question, given the uncertainty prior to the purchase program caused by GSE conservatorship and the financial crisis. Another study found small effects of the Fed's MBS purchases on interest rates after adjusting for prepayment and default risk, with the effect mainly occurring at the time the program was announced—before purchases had begun.[34]

Another fear that has been raised is that QE2 will lead to excessive risk taking by driving excess liquidity into riskier pursuits, possibly leading to another asset bubble. Arguably, more risk taking is needed in the economy today, as the financial crisis has left investors extremely risk averse. Given that QE1 seems to have had a relatively modest effects on yields, the risk of QE2 leading to bubbles does not seem acute at this time. Nevertheless, some see the role of monetary policy in last decade's housing bubble as a cautionary tale. Many economists have argued that the Fed left interest rates too low for too long after the last recession because of what turned out to be unfounded fears of deflation and a double dip recession. For example, the recession ended in November 2001, but the federal funds rate was not raised above 2% until the end of 2004. They believe that overly loose monetary policy contributed to the housing bubble by making too much credit available.

The Fed likely favors Treasury securities as the vehicle for quantitative easing because it has a neutral effect on the allocation of capital. (Its purchases of mortgage-related assets in QE1, on the other hand, would be expected to shift the market allocation of capital in favor of housing. One goal of QE1 was to stabilize a fragile housing market.)[35] The drawback of purchasing Treasury securities is that it may have less "bang for the buck" in terms of stimulating overall spending than if the Fed purchased an equivalent amount of private securities or made an equivalent amount of direct loans to private corporations. (Both of these options currently face statutory limitations.) The advantage of purchasing Treasury securities is that it does not put the Fed in the position of "picking winners," which it arguably is not set up to do as well as private financial markets. It could also undermine the Fed's political independence.

Exchange Rate Channel

Another channel through which quantitative easing could affect the economy is through effects on the value of the dollar. While influencing the exchange rate is not a stated goal of QE2, most macroeconomic models would predict, all else equal, that a byproduct of quantitative easing (or any monetary stimulus) would be to reduce the value of the dollar, assuming other countries do not alter their monetary policy in response.[36] Some critics have opposed QE2 on the grounds that it will reduce the value of the dollar, but in conventional models, a weaker dollar would have a stimulative effect on total spending by increasing exports and decreasing imports, all else equal. A decline in the trade deficit could help reduce "global imbalances" that some economists believe are a threat to global economic stability. If QE2 causes political friction that results in trading partners altering exchange rate or trade policies, however, that would also have an effect on the U.S. economy.

In real terms, after a downward trend since 2002, the broad inflation-adjusted dollar index rose from September 2008 until the spring of 2009, despite balance sheet expansion. Most economists attribute this to a "flight to quality" effect, as investors flocked to dollar-denominated assets as a safe haven despite the fact that the crisis was centered in U.S. mortgage markets. The dollar then declined from the announcement of the first large scale asset purchase program to the fall of 2009, and remained relatively stable over the following year. Exchange rate movements are determined by many factors besides monetary policy, including relative growth rates, inflation rates, saving rates, and investment rates. Furthermore, economic models are fairly unsuccessful in predicting exchange rate movements, so the forecasted path of the dollar remains relatively uncertain.

One study estimated that the dollar declined by an average of 3.71% against 5 major currencies following the Fed's March 2009 asset purchase announcement.[37] Including prior statements that foreshadowed the March 2009 announcement, the dollar fell by a cumulative 6.56%. The actual change in the dollar was somewhat smaller than the author's model had predicted. A shortcoming of this type of study is that a big jump in the dollar after the announcement could potentially be dissipated by subsequent market movements, leaving no substantial economic effect over time. Since the dollar continued to depreciate after March 2009, that does not seem to be the case.

EXIT STRATEGY

Once the economic outlook improves, banks may decide to use their reserve holdings to rapidly increase their lending. At that point, if the Fed found itself fighting inflationary pressures, it would have to find a way to prevent banks from lending those reserves to prevent an excessive increase in the money supply.[38] The most straightforward method to achieve this would be for the Fed to withdraw those reserves from the banking system by selling some of its assets or not replacing assets that mature. This would reduce both the assets and liabilities on its balance sheet. Some of the Fed's outstanding assets can be sold relatively quickly in theory, although there could be political resistance in reality. By April 2010, the Fed's balance sheet consisted predominantly of securities that could be sold in secondary markets. But the Fed has pledged to hold these assets long term. Given the Fed's concerns about the fragility of housing markets, it is not clear how its mortgage-related holdings could be reduced quickly if the Fed became concerned about rising inflation. Selling only Treasury securities might not be sufficient, given the size of the balance sheet compared to the amount of Treasury securities the Fed might feel comfortable selling. In 2008, the Fed was only comfortable reducing its holdings of Treasury securities to approximately $480 billion.

Another option would be to give banks incentives not to lend out reserves by raising the interest rate that the Fed pays on reserves, thereby keeping the larger monetary base from increasing the broader money supply.[39] Since there is no domestic and very little international experience with first increasing the monetary base and then tightening policy without reversing the increase in the monetary base, this strategy can be considered untested.[40] To better prevent these reserves from being lent out if necessary, the Fed began offering "term deposits" with a one to six month maturity for bank reserves. The interest rate on these term deposits would be set through auction; banks would presumably be willing to bid for term deposits only if the interest rate exceeded the rate paid by the Fed on normal reserves.

The Fed could also attempt to reduce liquidity by lending its assets out through "reverse repos."[41] This would change the composition of liabilities on the Fed's balance sheet, replacing its other liabilities with reverse repos. It is unlikely that reverse repos operations could be large enough to remove most of the new liquidity, however.[42]

Cash balances held at the Fed through the Treasury Supplemental Financing Program could also be used to tie up excess liquidity if needed. The Treasury announced the Supplementary Financing Program on September 17, 2008, as an alternative method for the Fed to increase its assistance to the financial sector without increasing the amount of money in circulation.[43] Under this program, the Treasury has temporarily auctioned more new securities than it needs to finance government operations and has deposited the proceeds at the Fed. (The operations do not affect inflation because the money received by the Treasury is held at the Fed and not allowed to circulate in the economy.) Since 2009, $200 billion has been kept in this account, except at times when the federal debt has approached the statutory debt limit. Given that the size of this program is constrained by the debt limit, it would be insufficient to significantly reduce liquidity without a large increase in the debt limit.[44]

If the Fed decides to pursue an exit strategy based on raising rates while maintaining a large balance sheet, economic theory casts some doubt on whether it would have any overall effect on the economy. Any stimulative effect of a larger balance sheet on the economy would be offset by the effects of paying interest on reserves, reverse repos, the Treasury Supplemental Program, or issuing Fed bonds. The large balance sheet would have no positive effect on aggregate demand if it is offset by any of these actions that drain liquidity from the economy.

If investors have rational expectations, it is not clear how this strategy could flatten the yield curve either, since the long end of the yield curve is determined primarily by expectations of future interest rates, and sterilized purchases of assets in the present should not change those expectations, all else equal. Previous experience suggests that sterilized attempts to flatten the yield curve have failed to stimulate the economy. For example, a study by Ben Bernanke (before he became Fed Chairman) and other economists concluded that a similar policy in the 1960s called "Operation Twist" is "widely viewed today as having been a failure."[45]

To date, quantitative easing has not had any noticeable effect on the public's inflationary expectations. If inflationary expectations remain low, it would be expected to make an exit strategy, and monetary policy generally, more effective. On the other hand, one criticism of quantitative easing is that it could undermine expectations of low and stable inflation, and the Fed's credibility on inflation. If inflationary expectations rise, larger-scale operations could become necessary for an exit strategy. In a worst case scenario, a rise in inflationary expectations could force the Fed to pursue an exit strategy before the economy has recovered, or risk "stagflation" (stagnant growth with high inflation).

SOME POSSIBLE CONGRESSIONAL CONCERNS

Impact on the Federal Budget Deficit

The Fed is a self-financing entity that yields a profit each year. That profit is largely remitted to the Treasury, where it is added to general revenues, thereby reducing the budget deficit.[46] As the Fed has increased the interest-earning assets on its balance sheet, its profits have increased. The Fed had net income of $38.8 billion and remitted $34.9 billion to the Treasury in 2008. Net income increased to $52.4 billion and remittances to the Treasury rose to $47.4 billion in 2009. A further $600 billion increase in Treasury security holdings would be expected to increase the Fed's profits further.

The Fed's profits are generated by the positive spread between its interest-earning assets (securities and loans) and its liabilities. Federal reserve notes are interest-free liabilities, and until 2008, bank reserves were also interest-free liabilities. Congress authorized the Fed to pay interest on bank reserves in the Emergency Economic Stabilization Act of 2008 (P.L. 110-343).[47] Since the Fed began paying interest on reserves in mid-October 2008, it has set the interest rate near the federal funds rate target, and has paid 0.25% on reserves since December 2008. Through the first half of 2010, the Fed has paid $4.4 billion in interest over the life of the program, reducing the Fed's net income by an equal amount. While the cost of paying interest on reserves is relatively low when interest rates are near zero, were the federal funds rate to return to a more normal level and reserves remained large—a scenario outlined in the section on "Exit Strategy"—it could significantly reduce the Fed's remittances to Treasury.[48]

The Treasury Supplemental Financing Program also has implications for the federal budget deficit. The Supplemental Financing Program requires Treasury to issue more interest-bearing securities, thereby increasing the government's debt service costs. Higher debt service costs are ultimately canceled out by higher profits on the Fed's larger holdings of Treasury securities, leaving the deficit no larger than if the Supplemental Financing Program were reduced to zero and the Fed reduced its assets by an equivalent amount. Nevertheless, the Supplemental Financing Program leaves the deficit larger than if the Fed's Treasury purchases were backed by higher bank reserves, as long as the interest paid on reserves is lower than Treasury yields.

Fears that the emergency activities of the Fed would lead to losses have proved to be unfounded. To date, the Fed has not realized any losses and relatively few risky assets (namely, the TALF loans and the Maiden Lane assets) remain on the balance sheet. While the Fed's exposure to Agency debt and Agency MBS remain high, these assets have no credit risk as long as the federal government stands behind the GSEs. Nonetheless, the Fed faces interest rate risk and prepayment risk on the assets. Losses on these assets could be realized in a scenario where interest rates rose and the Fed were forced to sell them. But if the Fed holds them to maturity, no losses should ever be realized.

Is the Fed Monetizing the Federal Deficit?

Some commentators have interpreted the Fed's decision to make large scale purchases of Treasury securities as a signal that the Fed intends to "monetize the federal deficit," which in 2009 reached its highest share of GDP since World War II, and remained at similar levels in 2010. Monetizing the deficit occurs when the budget deficit is financed by money creation rather than by selling bonds to private investors. Hyperinflation in foreign countries has consistently resulted from governments' decisions to monetize large deficits.

According to this definition, the deficit has not been monetized. Section 14 of the Federal Reserve Act legally forbids the Fed from buying newly issued securities directly from the Treasury, and all Treasury securities purchased by the Fed to date have been purchased on the secondary market, from private investors.[49] In modern times, the Fed has always held Treasury securities in order to conduct normal open market operations. Moreover, the size of the Fed's planned purchases of Treasury securities is small relative to the overall deficit. From fiscal years 2009 to 2011, the federal government is projected to run budget deficits equal to a cumulative $3.8 trillion, and the Fed has already purchased or is planning to purchase $600 billion of Treasury securities (plus a small amount to replace maturing MBS and GSE debt.)

Nonetheless, the effect of the Fed's purchase of Treasury securities on the federal budget is similar to monetization whether the Fed buys the securities on the secondary market or directly from Treasury. When the Fed holds Treasury securities, Treasury must pay interest to the Fed, just as it would pay interest to a private investor. These interest payments, after expenses, become profits to the Fed. The Fed, in turn, remits about 95% of its profits to the Treasury, where they are added to general revenues.[50] In essence, the Fed has made an interest-free loan to the Treasury, because almost all of the interest paid by Treasury to the Fed is subsequently sent back to Treasury.

The Fed could increase its profits and remittances to Treasury by printing more money to purchase more Treasury bonds (or any other asset). The Fed's profits are the incidental side effect of its open market operations in pursuit of its statutory mandate (to keep prices stable and unemployment low). If the Fed chose instead to buy assets with a goal of increasing its profits and remittances, it would be unlikely to meet its statutory mandate. The key practical difference between experiences that have been characterized as monetizing the deficit and the Fed's actions is that under the former, the goal of monetary policy becomes the financing of the government's budget deficit.

CONCLUSION

By December 2008, the Fed had reduced the federal funds rate to zero, thereby exhausting its ability to stimulate the economy through conventional policy. The Fed could have stopped there, but instead took a series of creative and aggressive unconventional policy actions to stimulate an economy that, following the financial crisis, experienced the deepest and longest recession since the Great Depression. QE2 took place in a somewhat different context—the recession had ended, and liquidity in key financial markets had been restored, but employment growth was still sluggish and inflation was close to zero.

QE2 can be thought of as QE1 on a smaller scale. Thus, assuming the economic context has not changed fundamentally, arguably the best way to predict the effects of QE2 is to look at the effects of QE1, and adjust them proportionately downward. The direct effect of QE1 was to increase excess bank reserves from almost zero to over $1 trillion, which, in essence, is how the Fed's loans and asset purchases were financed. In normal conditions, banks would be expected to lend out these reserves relatively quickly, which would boost economic growth and result in a rapid increase in the money supply through a money multiplier effect, that would increase inflation. Instead, bank lending fell 0.3% over the past year, and the doubling in the portion of the money supply controlled by the Fed (roughly equivalent to the growth in the Fed's balance sheet), did not translate into large increases in overall measures of the money supply. Some would point to the $1 trillion in bank reserves as evidence that quantitative easing is "pushing on a string."

Even if this bank lending channel does not work, the Fed has stressed that quantitative easing can still stimulate the economy through an interest rate channel. Purchasing Treasury securities of longer maturities should reduce long-term Treasury yields. But to stimulate the broader economy, two additional steps are necessary. First, it is necessary for the decline in interest rates to spread to private assets that were not purchased. Second, businesses and consumers must be willing and able to respond to lower interest rates by increase their interest-sensitive investment and consumption spending, respectively. Although interest rates did not fall after QE1 in absolute terms, most research indicates it resulted in a modest decrease in interest rates, relative to if the Fed had not purchased these assets, that modestly increased economic growth relative to what would have occurred in the absence of QE1.

Some critics have complained that QE2 will lead to a weaker dollar. Most macroeconomic models would predict that QE2 would lead to a weaker dollar, and this would stimulate the overall economy by stimulating net exports, assuming other central banks do not take steps that depreciate their currencies at the same time.

Though there is a consensus that the benefits of QE1 outweighed the risks, the Fed's decision to increase its balance sheet further through QE2 is less clear cut. The recession has officially ended, and the consensus forecast is that the economy will continue to grow in the next year. A case could be made that QE2 is not necessary because the economy is already on the road back to full employment, so the benefits of trying to get there a little faster do not outweigh the risks. On the other hand, although it is growing, the economy is expected to grow relatively slowly, and unemployment is expected to remain above 9% through the end of next year. Inflation is still close to zero, and has been falling. If this forecast is accurate, a case can be made that QE2 would be expected to help the Fed meet its dual mandate.

Furthermore, there are downside risks to the economy, which can be considered improbable, but not implausible. The economy could experience a "double dip" into another recession. Alternatively, it could keep growing, but not quickly enough to return to full employment or keep prices from falling. In other words, it could fall into a "deflationary trap" of the type experienced by Japan after its asset bubble collapsed, where unemployment rose for 11 consecutive years and prices fell in 10 out of 14 years. The lesson from Japan seems to be that conventional fiscal and monetary stimulus that would be considered fairly aggressive in normal conditions are not enough to overcome a deflationary trap, particularly if withdrawn prematurely. Japan even tried quantitative easing on a smaller scale than QE1 from 2001 to 2006, and was unable to generate more than modest economic growth and inflation. QE2 could be seen as insurance against a double dip recession or deflationary trap, and if the economy were to experience either, the worst that might be said about it is that its effects would be too small to make a difference.

While those predicting a double dip and deflationary trap are in the minority, there are arguably even fewer economists who are predicting that the economy will grow so rapidly next year that high inflation will become a problem. Nevertheless, a lesson that could be taken from the last recession is it can be dangerous to leave monetary policy too loose for too long. There is a risk that QE2 will eventually lead to excessive inflation because it leads to an increase in bank reserves. Eventually, banks may decide to use those reserves to rapidly increase lending, in which case the growth in the monetary base would translate into a large increase in the overall money supply.

The Fed has acknowledged this risk and has devoted considerable efforts to developing an "exit strategy" from quantitative easing when appropriate. But will the exit strategy work? The most straightforward exit strategy would be for the Fed to sell its assets, thereby automatically reversing the growth in its balance sheet and the money supply. The Fed seems somewhat reluctant to pursue this strategy as long as the housing market remains fragile because it would likely involve the sale of its mortgage-related assets. Its other main proposal is to give banks an incentive to keep those reserves sitting at the Fed by raising the interest it pays on reserves, a power that Congress granted the Fed in 2008. This approach is largely untested in the United States or abroad, so its potential effectiveness is unproven. At current reserve levels, it would involve considerable expenditure if interest rates returned to levels closer to their long-term averages, and that expense would ultimately be borne by the taxpayer, since it would reduce the Fed's profits, which are mostly remitted to the Treasury.

End Notes

[1] In this report, actions taken by the Federal Reserve Board, the Federal Open Market Committee, or a Federal Reserve regional bank are all referred to as the Federal Reserve.

[2] For these purposes, agency debt includes the debt securities of Fannie Mae, Freddie Mac, and the Federal Home Loan Banks. Agency MBS includes MBS issued by Fannie Mae, Freddie Mac, and Ginnie Mae.

[3] Since the Civil War, short-term interest rates approached zero only in the Great Depression. For much of the Great Depression, the Fed pursued policies that made the money supply contract. James Clouse et al, "Monetary Policy When the Nominal Short-Term Interest Rate is Zero," *Topics in Macroeconomics*, vol. 3, no. 1, 2003; Allan Meltzer, *A History of the Federal Reserve*, vol. 1 (Chicago: University of Chicago Press, 2003).

[4] Federal Reserve Act, Section 2A, 12 USC 225a.

[5] Federal Open Market Committee, Federal Reserve, "press release," November 3, 2010, http://www.federalreserve.gov/newsevents/press/monetary/20101103a.htm.

[6] The letter can be accessed at http://economics21.org/commentary/e21s-open-letter-ben-bernanke.

[7] For more information on these facilities, see CRS Report R41073, *Government Interventions in Response to Financial Turmoil*, by Baird Webel and Marc Labonte.

[8] All data on direct lending and support for institutions downloaded from http://www.federalreserve.gov/ monetarypolicy/bst_recenttrends.htm. Hereafter, these data will be referred to as "emergency lending."

[9] Federal Open Market Committee, Federal Reserve, "press release," March 18, 2009, http://www.federalreserve.gov/ newsevents/press/monetary/20090318a.htm. For these purposes, agency debt includes the debt securities of Fannie Mae, Freddie Mac, and the Federal Home Loan Banks. Agency MBS includes MBS issued by Fannie Mae, Freddie Mac, and Ginnie Mae.

[10] Chairman Ben Bernanke, "The Federal Reserve's Balance Sheet: An Update," Speech at the Federal Reserve Board Conference on Key Developments in Monetary Policy, October 8, 2009.

[11] Federal Open Market Committee, Federal Reserve, "press release," August 10, 2010, http://www.federalreserve.gov/ newsevents/press/monetary/20100810a.htm.

[12] Federal Reserve Bank of New York, "Statement Regarding Purchases of Treasury Securities," November 3, 2010.

[13] For more information, see CRS Report RL30354, *Monetary Policy and the Federal Reserve: Current Policy and Conditions*, by Marc Labonte.

[14] Federal Open Market Committee, Federal Reserve, "press release," November 3, 2010.

[15] See, for example, *Blue Chip Economic Indicators*, vol. 35, no. 11, November 11, 2010.

[16] The economy experienced two recessions during the Great Depression. The first ended in 1933 and the second began in 1937. The Great Depression experience is not comparable to current fears of a double dip recession because the two recessions were over four years apart, and output grew very rapidly during the expansion between the two recessions. For more information, see CRS Report R41444, *Double-Dip Recession: Previous Experience and Current Prospect*, by Craig K. Elwell.

[17] For more information, see CRS Report R40512, *Deflation: Economic Significance, Current Risk, and Policy Responses*, by Craig K. Elwell.

[18] Murtaza Syed et al., "Lost Decade in Translation: What Japan's Crisis Could Portend About Recovery from the Great Recession," International Monetary Fund, working paper 09/282, December 2009.

[19] Chairman Bernanke defines the informal "comfort zone" as 1% to 2% inflation. See, for example, Ben S. Bernanke, Remarks at a Finance Committee luncheon of the Executives' Club of Chicago, Chicago, Illinois, March 8, 2005.

[20] For example the private firm Blue Chip surveys 50 private sector economic forecasters each month. In its November forecast, the ten most pessimistic forecasters on average projected that GDP would rise by 1.9% and the CPI would rise by 1.1% in 2011. The ten most optimistic forecasters on average projected that GDP would rise by 2.9% and CPI would rise by 2.0%.

[21] Donald Kohn, "Interactions Between Monetary and Fiscal Policy in the Current Situation," speech at Princeton University, Princeton, NJ, May 23, 2009.

[22] Jan Hatzius and Sven Stehn, "QE2: How Much is Needed?" *U.S. Economics Analyst*, Goldman Sachs, October 22, 2010; Sven Stehn, "QE2 Sets Sail With Favorable Winds," *U.S. Economics Analyst*, Goldman Sachs, November 5, 2010.

[23] Reported in "Down the Slipway," *The Economist*, November 6, 2010, p. 89.

[24] Some commentators have argued that banks will use these reserves to speculate on securities, but banks' securities holdings have risen by less than $200 billion (8%) in the last year. Bank data cover all FDIC-insured institutions and are taken from Federal Deposit Insurance Corporation, *Quarterly Banking Profile*, vol. 4, no. 3, 2010, Table II-A.

[25] Inflation has been low and stable in the last 25 years in part because the Fed has periodically raised interest rates to contain inflationary pressures and has not allowed the money supply to grow rapidly.

[26] Quantitative easing was found to have similar effects on lending and inflation occurred in Japan. See Hiroshi Ugai, "Effects of the Quantitative Easing Policy: A Survey of Empirical Analyses," Bank of Japan, working paper no. 06-E10, July 2006.

[27] See, for example, Chairman Ben Bernanke, "What the Fed Did and Why," *Washington Post*, November 5, 2010.

[28] Glenn Rudebusch, *The Fed's Exit Strategy for Monetary Policy*, Federal Reserve Bank of San Francisco, Economic Letter 2010-18, June 2010.

[29] It is also possible that this channel could stimulate the economy through a wealth effect, since lower yields would be expected to raise the value of securities. If this made the holders of these securities feel more wealthy, it could stimulate their consumption spending.

[30] There is little past experience to analyze in the United States, as quantitative easing had never previously been undertaken. In the 1960s, the Fed attempted to flatten the yield curve through sterilized Treasury purchases through a policy referred to as "Operation Twist," that was not financed through quantitative easing. A study by Ben Bernanke (before he was Fed chairman) and other economists concluded that "Operation Twist" is "widely viewed today as having been a failure." Ben Bernanke, Vincent Reinhart, and Brian Sack, "Monetary Policy Alternatives at the Zero Bound," Federal Reserve Board of Governors, *Finance and Economics Discussion Series 2004-48*, 2004, p. 28. A survey of studies on Japan's quantitative easing found the asset yield "effects, if any, were small..." See Hiroshi Ugai, "Effects of the Quantitative Easing Policy: A Survey of Empirical Analyses," Bank of Japan, working paper no. 06-E10, July 2006, p. 44.

[31] See, for example, Sven Stehn, "QE2: How Much Has Been Priced In?," *U.S. Daily*, newsletter, Goldman Sachs, October 7, 2010.

[32] Joseph Gagnon et al., "Large-Scale Asset Purchases by the Federal Reserve: Did They Work?" Federal Reserve Bank of New York, *Staff Reports*, no. 441, March 2010. See also James Hamilton and Jing Wu, "The Effectiveness of Alternative Monetary Policy Tools in a Zero Lower Bound Environment," University of California San Diego, working paper, October 2, 2010. This study estimates that a $400 billion purchase of long-term Treasury securities would reduce Treasury yields by 0.14 percentage points. In their model, whether or not the purchases are financed through quantitative easing does not change the results.

[33] Stefania D'Amico and Thomas King, "Flow and Stock Effects of Large-Scale Treasury Purchases," Federal Reserve Board, *Finance and Economics Discussion Series*, no. 52, September 2010. The authors' results were only statistically significant when they assumed (and controlled for the assumption) that the Fed was purchasing underpriced securities, however.

[34] Johannes Stroebel and John Taylor, "Estimated Impact of the Fed's Mortgage-Backed Securities Purchase Program," National Bureau of Economic Research, working paper 15626, December 2009.

[35] Federal Open Market Committee, Federal Reserve, "press release," March 18, 2009.

[36] Countries that intervene to keep their exchange rate from appreciating against the dollar may be forced to match U.S. monetary expansion in order to maintain their exchange rate goals.

[37] Christopher Neely, *The Large-Scale Asset Purchases Had Large International Effects*, Federal Reserve Bank of St. Louis, working paper 2010-018B, October 2010.

[38] The Fed's views on the issues outlined in this section can be read in Ben Bernanke, "The Fed's Exit Strategy," *Wall Street Journal*, July 21, 2009, p. A15. See also Claudio Borio and Piti Disyatat, *Unconventional Monetary Policies: An Appraisal*," Bank for International Settlements, Working Paper 292, November 2009; John Taylor, "An Exit Rule for Monetary Policy," Testimony before the Committee on Financial Services, U.S. House of Representatives, March 25, 2010.

[39] Economist Alan Blinder argues that the interest on reserves can help ensure that an exit strategy of selling assets is not disruptive. Alan Blinder, "Quantitative Easing: Entrance and Exit Strategies," *Federal Reserve Bank of St. Louis Review*, vol. 92, no. 6, November 2010, p. 465.

[40] One paper looks at international experience with paying interest on bank reserves to answer this question. There is very limited experience with raising short-term interest rates while maintaining excess reserve balances, however. Japan in the 1990s is the best-known case of quantitative easing, and it removed excess balances before raising rates. The authors found that Norway had successfully raised rates while maintaining excess reserves from 2005 to 2008, although they did reduce reserves by half during that period. David Bowman, Etienne Gagnon, Mike Leahy, "Interest on Excess Reserves as a Monetary Policy Instrument: The Experience of Foreign Central Banks," Federal Reserve Board, *International Finance Discussion Paper 996*, March 2010. See also Richard Anderson et al., "Doubling Your Monetary Base and Surviving: Some International Experience," *Federal Reserve Bank of St. Louis Review*, vol. 92, no. 6, November 2010, p. 481.

[41] A reverse repo (or reverse repurchase agreement) is a purchase of securities with an agreement to resell them at a higher price at a specific future date. The transaction is equivalent to a loan, with the securities serving as collateral.

[42] The size of reverse repo operations are limited to the amount of securities held by the Fed available to lend and private investors' willingness to borrow them. In recent years, reverse repos outstanding have not exceeded $108 billion. Goldman Sachs reports that Fed officials have indicated that they do not believe private investors could absorb more than $100 billion in reverse repos. Ed McKelvey, "Fed Lays Groundwork to Offset Another Increase in Excess Reserves," *U.S. Daily Newsletter*, September 24, 2009.

[43] The Treasuries issued under the program are indistinguishable to investors from regularly-issued securities.

[44] The Fed and Treasury announced in March 2009 that they would seek "legislative action to provide additional tools the Federal Reserve can use to sterilize the effects of its lending or securities purchases on the supply of bank reserves." Many analysts interpreted this statement to express the desire for the Fed to gain authority to issue its own bonds. To date, legislation to allow the Fed to do so has not been considered, and the idea has not been widely discussed since.

[45] Ben Bernanke, Vincent Reinhart, and Brian Sack, "Monetary Policy Alternatives at the Zero Bound," Federal Reserve Board of Governors, *Finance and Economics Discussion Series 2004-48*, 2004, p. 28.

[46] Other profits are paid out to stockholders and added to the Fed's surplus as a buffer against potential losses.

[47] This authority was originally allowed beginning in 2011 in the Financial Services Regulatory Relief Act of 2006 (P.L. 109-351). The Emergency Economic Stabilization Act of 2008 granted immediate authority.

[48] For example, if reserves held at the Fed equaled $1 trillion and the rate paid on reserves was set at 5%, the Fed would pay $50 billion of interest on reserves over a year.

[49] Until 1978, the Treasury had limited authority to "draw" from the Fed to finance its deficits, and used that authority sparingly. U.S. Congress, House Committee on Banking, Finance, and Urban Affairs, Domestic Monetary Policy, *Extending the Treasury-Federal Reserve Draw Authority*, committee print, 95th Cong., 2nd sess., April 5, 1978, 26-179 (Washington: GPO, 1978).

[50] The net addition to general revenues is reduced by the extra interest the Treasury must pay on debt it issued in order to deposit cash at the Fed.

In: The Federal Reserve
Editor: John P. Ranchett

ISBN: 978-1-62100-528-5
© 2011 Nova Science Publishers, Inc.

Chapter 7

REMARKS BY BEN S. BERNANKE, CHAIRMAN, BOARD OF GOVERNORS OF THE FEDERAL RESERVE SYSTEM, AT THE FEDERAL RESERVE BANK OF CHICAGO, 47TH ANNUAL CONFERENCE ON BANK STRUCTURE AND COMPETITION, HEARING ON "IMPLEMENTING A MACROPRUDENTIAL APPROACH TO SUPERVISION AND REGULATION"[*]

The recent financial crisis revealed critical gaps and weaknesses in the U.S. financial system and the financial regulatory framework. The Congress and the Administration last year provided a roadmap for addressing many of these problems, in the form of the Dodd-Frank Wall Street Reform and Consumer Protection Act (Dodd-Frank Act)--the topic of this year's conference.

Legislative reforms in any complex area always face the risk of fighting the last war, responding to the causes of the last crisis without sufficient

---

[*] This is an edited, reformatted and augmented version of remarks given by Ben S. Bernanke, Chairman, Board of Governors of the Federal Reserve System, at the Federal Reserve Bank of Chicago, 47th Annual Conference on Bank Structure and Competition, Hearing on "Implementing a Macroprudential Approach to Supervision and Regulation" on May 5, 2011.

attention to where new problems may arise. To their credit, the authors of the Dodd-Frank Act attempted to reduce this risk by building in a number of features aimed at helping our system of financial oversight adapt over time to changes in the financial environment. Notably, a central element of the legislation is the requirement that the Federal Reserve and other financial regulatory agencies adopt a so-called macroprudential approach--that is, an approach that supplements traditional supervision and regulation of individual firms or markets with explicit consideration of threats to the stability of the financial system as a whole. The act also created a new Financial Stability Oversight Council, whose membership comprises a diverse group of federal and state financial regulators, to coordinate the government's efforts to identify and respond to systemic risks.

The explicit incorporation of macroprudential considerations in the nation's framework for financial oversight represents a major innovation in our thinking about financial regulation, one that is taking hold abroad as well as in the United States. This new direction is constructive and necessary, I believe, but it also poses considerable conceptual and operational challenges in its implementation. In my remarks today I will briefly discuss the rationale for macroprudential supervision and regulation, describe the new structure of macroprudential supervision and regulation in the United States, and explain how we at the Fed are doing our part to implement the macroprudential approach to financial oversight.

MACROPRUDENTIAL SUPERVISION AND REGULATION

Ultimately, the goal of macroprudential supervision and regulation is to minimize the risk of financial disruptions that are sufficiently severe to inflict significant damage on the broader economy. The systemic orientation of the macroprudential approach may be contrasted with that of the traditional, or "microprudential," approach to regulation and supervision, which is concerned primarily with the safety and soundness of individual institutions, markets, or infrastructures.

Relative to traditional regulation and supervision, executing a macroprudential approach to oversight can involve heavier informational requirements and more-complex analytic frameworks. In particular, because of the highly interconnected nature of our financial system, macroprudential oversight must be concerned with all major segments of the financial sector, including financial institutions, markets, and infrastructures; it must also place particular emphasis on understanding the complex linkages and interdependencies among institutions and markets, as these linkages determine how instability may be propagated throughout the system. Moreover, broadly speaking, macroprudential regulators must be concerned with at least two types of risks. The first type encompasses aspects of the structure of the financial system--such as gaps in regulatory coverage or the evolution of shadow banking--that pose ongoing risks to financial stability. The second class of risks are those that vary over time with financial or economic circumstances, such as widespread buildups of leverage in good times that could ultimately unwind in destabilizing ways.

To be sure, a macroprudential approach to oversight does not avoid the need for careful microprudential regulation and supervision. The oversight of individual institutions serves many purposes beyond the enhancement of systemic stability, including the protection of the deposit insurance fund, the detection of money laundering and other forms of financial crime, and the prevention of unlawful discrimination or abusive lending practices. Equally important, however, is that microprudential oversight also provides the knowledge base on which a more systemic approach must be built; we cannot understand what is going on in the system as a whole without a clear view of developments within key firms and markets. Without a strong microprudential framework to underpin them, macroprudential policies would be ineffective.

That said, a key lesson of the crisis is that a purely microprudential approach, focused on the conditions of individual firms or markets, may fail to detect important systemic or cross-cutting risks. For example, a traditional microprudential examination might find that an individual financial institution is relying heavily on short-term wholesale funding, which may or may not induce a supervisory response. The implications of that finding for the stability of the broader system, however, cannot be determined without knowing what is happening outside that particular firm. Are other, similar financial firms also highly reliant on short-term funding? If so, are the sources of short-term funding heavily concentrated? Is the market for short-term funding likely to be stable in a period of high uncertainty, or is it vulnerable to runs? If short-term funding were suddenly to become unavailable, how would the borrowing firms react—for example, would they be forced into a fire sale of assets, which itself could be destabilizing, or would they cease to provide funding or critical services for other financial actors? Finally, what implications would these developments have for the broader economy? The analysis of risks from a systemic perspective, not just from the perspective of an individual firm, is the hallmark of macroprudential regulation and supervision. And the remedies that might emerge from such an analysis could well be more far-reaching and more structural in nature than simply requiring a few firms to modify their funding patterns.

IMPLEMENTING THE MACROPRUDENTIAL APPROACH IN THE UNITED STATES

Let me be more concrete and talk about the implementation of the macroprudential approach in the context of the evolving U.S. regulatory system.

The first required element of macroprudential oversight is a system for monitoring evolving risks to financial stability. Beyond assigning individual regulatory agencies this responsibility, the Dodd-Frank Act took the additional step of setting up a new body, the Financial Stability Oversight Council, as I mentioned earlier. The council is charged with monitoring the U.S. financial system, identifying risks that threaten the stability of that system, and promoting market discipline and other conditions that mitigate excessive risk-taking in financial markets. The council is made up of 10 voting members--including the Federal Reserve--and 5 nonvoting members, who serve in an advisory capacity.[1]

The regulatory agencies represented on the council oversee a wide range of participants in the U.S. financial system. The broad membership of the council is intended to limit the tendency of regulators to focus narrowly on the institutions and markets within their jurisdictions while overlooking risks from interdependencies that cut across jurisdictions. The council also facilitates coordination and information sharing among member agencies. By breaking down the silos that in the past sometimes discouraged agencies from looking beyond their specific responsibilities, the council should help identify and eliminate gaps and weaknesses within the regulatory structure.

The Dodd-Frank Act also established--within the Treasury Department--the Office of Financial Research, which is responsible for improving the quality of financial data available to policymakers. The oversight council may direct the research office to collect information from certain individual financial companies to assess risks to the financial system. This collection and analysis of financial-sector data should allow regulators to see more of the financial landscape and better equip them to identify systemic risks and other emerging threats.

To digress for a moment, it's interesting that the United States isn't the only jurisdiction that has recently created a new institutional structure to implement macroprudential policies. Notably, the European Union (EU) established the European Systemic Risk Board, which is responsible for the macroprudential oversight of the EU's financial system. The board will collect and analyze information on the EU's financial system, identify and prioritize systemic risks, and issue warnings and recommendations to national and European authorities. It will also work closely with the three newly created European Supervisory Authorities, which in turn are charged with coordinating prudential regulations for banking, insurance, and securities among EU member states.[2] In the United Kingdom, the government plans to move its microprudential regulatory authority back into the Bank of England and create a new Financial Policy Committee to implement macroprudential policies. (Former Federal Reserve Board Vice Chairman Donald Kohn has been tapped to serve on the Financial Policy Committee, which must make him one of the few people to have served as a top financial regulator in two different countries.) The U.K. committee is expected to identify and monitor systemic risks and take actions to remove or reduce them. And it will operate a new resolution regime for failing financial firms.

The monitoring efforts of the Financial Stability Oversight Council in the United States are already well under way. Staff members from the member agencies have established working groups with responsibility for specific sectors or aspects of the financial system and are making regular presentations to the council. This work will also be reflected in the council's required annual report to the Congress on financial stability, which is expected to be released in the summer.

Of course, the identification of threats to financial stability must be followed by appropriate remedies. The powers of the council itself are relatively limited in this regard, at least under most circumstances. Perhaps its most important responsibility is the designation of certain nonbank financial firms and financial market utilities as systemically important and thereby subject to additional regulation and oversight by the Federal Reserve and other member agencies, including the Commodity Futures Trading Commission and the Securities and Exchange Commission (SEC). To make those designations, the council will need to determine criteria for identifying firms whose financial distress would impose the greatest risks to financial stability. Of course, this task requires continued development of an analytical framework for understanding systemic risk and its sources.

Although the council's own powers are circumscribed to some degree, the potential benefits of its ability to foster cooperative work among U.S. regulatory agencies should not be underestimated. To cite just one example, the stability of money market mutual funds--which suffered dramatic runs that worsened funding conditions at the height of the crisis--is clearly a systemic issue, not just an industry issue. The SEC, which has already issued rules to increase the stability of money market mutual funds, is appropriately taking the lead in investigating whether further steps are necessary. Under the aegis of the council, however, the SEC has consulted with other agencies, including the Federal Reserve, which have provided their own analyses and perspectives. In particular, interagency consultation has helped clarify the potential systemic implications of instability in the money market mutual fund industry. The Federal Reserve will be among the agencies participating in a roundtable on money fund regulation sponsored by the SEC later this month.

Understandably, given the damage wrought by the crisis, the council and its members remain focused on addressing possible sources of financial instability, including both structural problems and risks arising from ongoing economic or financial developments. However, no one's interests are served by the imposition of ineffective or burdensome rules that lead to excessive increases in costs or unnecessary restrictions in the supply of credit. Increased coordination and cooperation among regulators, under the auspices of the council where appropriate, should serve not only to improve our management of systemic risk, but also reduce the extent of duplicative, inconsistent, or ineffective rulemakings. More generally, in evaluating alternative approaches to mitigating systemic risks, regulators must aim to avoid stifling reasonable risk-taking and innovation in financial markets, as these factors play an important role in fostering broader productivity gains, economic growth, and job creation.

MACROPRUDENTIAL POLICY
AT THE FEDERAL RESERVE

As I have mentioned, besides creating new institutions like the Financial Stability Oversight Council, the Dodd-Frank Act has also imposed a macroprudential mandate on individual agencies, including the Federal Reserve. This mandate comes, in some cases, with changes in the powers and responsibilities of key agencies. In the case of the Federal Reserve, in addition to membership on the Financial Stability Oversight Council, our new responsibilities include the supervision of thrift holding companies as well as oversight of nonbank financial firms and certain payment, clearing, and settlement utilities that the council designates as systemically important. In consultation with other agencies, we also are responsible for developing more-stringent prudential standards for all large banking organizations and for nonbank firms designated by the council as systemically important. These enhanced standards include tougher capital and liquidity requirements, the development of resolution plans (so-called living wills), mandatory stress tests conducted by the Federal Reserve and by the firms themselves, new counterparty credit limits, and more-demanding risk-management requirements.

The Federal Reserve has made and will continue to make significant organizational changes as needed to best fulfill our responsibilities. Even before the enactment of the Dodd-Frank Act, we had begun to overhaul our supervision of the largest, most-complex financial firms. An important milestone in this regard was the Federal Reserve's leadership in the spring of 2009 of the Supervisory Capital Assessment Program, popularly known as the bank stress test, which comprehensively evaluated the health of the largest banking organizations in the country. We learned valuable lessons from that exercise, including an appreciation of the additional insights that can be gained by examining a number of major institutions simultaneously, with a focus on comparative performance. Another lesson of the stress test was the value of a multidisciplinary approach to supervision, one that combines the skills of economists, financial experts, payments systems analysts, and other specialists with those of supervisors and examiners.

Drawing on this experience, we created a high-level, multidisciplinary working group within the Federal Reserve to oversee the supervision of large financial institutions. Under the auspices of this committee--called the Large Institution Supervision Coordinating Committee, or LISCC--Federal Reserve supervisors, supported by economists and other experts, now routinely use horizontal, or cross-firm, reviews to monitor industry practices, common investment or funding strategies, changes in the degree or form of financial interconnectedness, or other developments with implications for systemic risk. Supplementing its individual and horizontal reviews, the LISCC has also made increasing use of improved quantitative methods for evaluating the health and performance of supervised firms as well as the risks they may pose to the broader financial system. A similar committee structure within the Federal

Reserve is being developed to help us meet our obligations to supervise systemically important financial market utilities.

To improve our monitoring of the financial system and to coordinate work bearing on financial stability, we have also created a new office within the Board, called the Office of Financial Stability Policy and Research. This office brings together staff with a range of backgrounds and skills and works closely with other groups at the Federal Reserve. The office helps monitor global financial risks and analyze the implications of those risks for financial stability; works with our bank supervisory committees, for example, on the development of quantitative loss models and alternative scenarios to serve as the basis for stress tests; serves as a liaison to the Financial Stability Oversight Council and its various working groups; and helps develop and evaluate alternative approaches to implementing macroprudential regulations.

The recent Comprehensive Capital Analysis and Review, in which the Federal Reserve evaluated the internal capital planning processes and shareholder distribution requests of the 19 largest bank holding companies, is an example of a horizontal assessment with a macroprudential approach. In the wake of the crisis, banks' capital payouts had been kept to a minimum. As banks' earnings and capital positions continued to improve in 2010, however, some firms sought approval to increase dividends or restart share repurchase programs. The simultaneous assessment of the payout requests in the capital review allowed the Federal Reserve, working through the LISCC, to evaluate not only the conditions of individual banks but also the potential implications of capital payouts for aggregate credit extension and the sustainability of the economic recovery. Thus, the program had both microprudential and macroprudential goals. From a traditional safety-and-soundness perspective, we wanted each firm to demonstrate that it had robust risk-management systems as well as a capital plan that would allow it to manage potential losses in stress scenarios while comfortably meeting Basel III capital requirements as they are phased in. But, with the help of macroeconomic and capital market analysts, we also considered the implications of the requests for the capital available to the banking system as a whole, with the objective of ensuring that bank credit would still be available to households and businesses even if the economy were to perform more poorly than expected.

We now also routinely apply macroprudential methods to the analysis of significant economic developments, whether domestic or foreign. The sovereign debt concerns in Europe provide one example. As yields on European sovereign debt and bank debt rose in the spring of 2010, Federal Reserve supervisors began to evaluate U.S. banking firms' exposures to

European banking firms and sovereigns. In addition to evaluating direct exposures, we analyzed scenarios under which sovereign debt concerns might lead to broader financial volatility. Our focus was on the possibility that financial disruptions might impede credit flows and economic activity in both Europe and the United States. In our work we conferred extensively with European bank supervisors; for example, we discussed potential risks to European banks' abilities to obtain dollar funding and the implications of European banks' need for dollars on U.S. money markets. This work suggested that providing a backstop for the dollar-funding needs of European financial institutions could mitigate the potential for spillovers to the United States from European sovereign debt concerns. In accord with this analysis, in May 2010 the Federal Open Market Committee announced that it had authorized dollar liquidity swap lines with other central banks in a preemptive move to avert a further deterioration in liquidity conditions.

Macroprudential considerations have also been important for the Federal Reserve's rulemaking, particularly those rules implementing the Dodd-Frank Act. For example, with other regulators, we recently proposed rules to set margin requirements for over-the-counter derivatives that are not cleared through a central counterparty. The proposed rules reflect not only safety-and-soundness concerns but also macroprudential goals; specifically, the rules seek to increase the resiliency of the financial system as a whole by reducing the potential for contagion between swap market participants. Under the proposed rules, the most-stringent margin requirements would apply to derivatives contracts between swap dealers or other major swaps market participants, as such arrangements could otherwise involve a risk of "default chains" in which distress at one major firm could cascade through the swap markets.

As I mentioned earlier, the macroprudential approach to financial regulation is gaining increasing adherence internationally. Along with our efforts to implement reforms domestically, the Federal Reserve has for some time been working closely with foreign counterparts to help coordinate the reform process at the international level. The objectives of international coordination are of the highest importance. These goals include maintaining a level competitive playing field across countries, minimizing opportunities for multinational firms to take advantage of weaker or inconsistent regulations in some jurisdictions, establishing consistent and complementary standards, and ensuring effective oversight of internationally active firms and markets. The Group of Twenty has devoted considerable attention to financial-sector policies in its meetings during the past couple of years. The Financial Stability Board, the Basel Committee on Banking Supervision, and other international groups also have undertaken substantial work to coordinate macroprudential policies across borders.

Much of the Federal Reserve's international effort has involved working with other regulatory agencies and central banks to design and implement new prudential requirements for internationally active banks. This work resulted in the adoption of more-stringent regulatory capital standards for trading activities and securitization exposures in the summer of 2009, as well as the agreement last fall on the major elements of the new Basel III framework for globally active banks. Consistent with the macroprudential approach, the Basel III framework requires the largest, most globally active banks to hold more, higher-quality capital, reflecting the greater systemic risk associated with financial distress at the largest institutions.

CONCLUSION

The financial crisis demonstrated clearly that supervisory and regulatory practices must consider overall financial stability as well as the safety and soundness of individual firms. The Dodd-Frank Act requires regulators to mitigate the buildup of financial excesses and reduce vulnerabilities, and it created an interagency council to monitor financial markets, to identify emerging threats, and to help formulate policies to contain those risks. For our part, the Federal Reserve has restructured its internal operations to facilitate a macroprudential approach to supervision and regulation and to monitor systemic risks. We are committed to working closely with the oversight council and other agencies to promote financial stability. While a great deal has been accomplished since the act was passed less than a year ago, much work remains to better understand sources of systemic risk, to develop improved monitoring tools, and to evaluate and implement policy instruments to reduce macroprudential risks. These are difficult challenges, but if we are to avoid a repeat of the crisis and its economic consequences, these challenges must be met.

End Notes

[1] The Secretary of the Treasury serves as the chairman of the Financial Stability Oversight Council. Other voting members include the heads of the Office of the Comptroller of the Currency, the Securities and Exchange Commission, the Federal Deposit Insurance Corporation, the Commodity Futures Trading Commission, the Federal Housing Finance Agency, the National Credit Union Administration, the Bureau of Consumer Financial Protection, and an independent insurance expert appointed by the President. The latter two seats are not yet filled.

[2] The three authorities are the European Securities and Markets Authority, the European Banking Authority, and the European Insurance and Occupational Pensions Authority.

INDEX

"

"speech", 31

2

2001 recession, 19, 21, 22, 69
20th century, 50, 100

A

access, 22, 106
accommodation, 90
accountability, 7, 28, 35, 47, 49, 51, 52, 56, 66, 75, 77, 78, 79, 80, 83
accounting, 26, 48, 53
adjustment, 18, 38, 44, 64
agencies, ix, 5, 47, 53, 74, 122, 124, 125, 126, 130
aggregate demand, 14, 18, 21, 22, 25, 33, 38, 39, 44, 45, 49, 89, 101, 111
aggregate supply, 38
agriculture, 6
alters, 86
analytical framework, 125
anchoring, 60
appointees, 42
appointments, 2
appropriations, 2

arrest, 70
assessment, 128
assets, 7, 14, 15, 16, 24, 25, 27, 29, 36, 67, 69, 96, 97, 98, 99, 101, 105, 106, 108, 109, 110, 111, 112, 113, 114, 116, 118, 123
asymmetry, 41
audit, 8, 9, 10, 12, 14, 26, 47, 53
authorities, 23, 34, 59, 125, 131
authority, 4, 5, 8, 9, 10, 14, 38, 51, 60, 71, 73, 74, 80, 119, 125
automobiles, 17, 38

B

bail, 73
balance sheet, ix, 4, 12, 24, 25, 70, 71, 93, 95, 96, 97, 99, 101, 103, 104, 109, 110, 111, 112, 114, 115, 116
Bank of England, 50, 125
bankers, 4, 17, 50
banking, 2, 4, 5, 6, 8, 12, 13, 23, 25, 35, 38, 94, 98, 105, 109, 123, 125, 127, 128
banking industry, 8
banks, iv, vii, 1, 2, 4, 5, 6, 7, 9, 11, 12, 13, 15, 16, 23, 24, 25, 27, 29, 36, 37, 43, 47, 50, 56, 57, 58, 59, 63, 67, 73, 94, 96, 104, 109, 110, 114, 115, 116, 117, 128, 129, 130

barriers, 67
base, 15, 25, 75, 98, 104, 110, 115, 123
BEA, 77
benefits, 25, 31, 34, 44, 46, 50, 51, 53, 56, 60, 61, 62, 64, 76, 105, 115, 126
beverages, 87
bias, 43, 61, 62, 107
blame, 30, 68
board members, 3
Board of Governors, iv, vi, vii, viii, 1, 2, 3, 4, 5, 6, 7, 8, 9, 10, 13, 25, 27, 31, 33, 34, 36, 43, 46, 57, 118, 119, 121
boils, 34, 46, 52
bonds, 6, 40, 106, 111, 113, 119
borrowers, 9, 20, 27, 73, 104
budget deficit, 18, 19, 20, 39, 44, 46, 71, 94, 95, 101, 111, 112, 113
Bureau of Labor Statistics, 77, 88
business cycle, 17, 19, 21, 28, 30, 34, 41, 43, 45, 61, 63, 86
businesses, 12, 13, 14, 16, 76, 86, 101, 114, 128

C

capital account, 37
capital flows, 20, 39
capital goods, 13, 16, 38
capital markets, 17
capital outflow, 20
cash, 11, 14, 15, 25, 119
casting, viii, 85
central bank, vii, 1, 2, 13, 15, 17, 29, 41, 43, 44, 46, 50, 56, 57, 59, 63, 67, 101, 115, 129, 130
challenges, 122, 130
checks and balances, 44
Chicago, vi, 6, 30, 53, 81, 92, 116, 117, 121
circulation, 6, 37, 110
City, 6, 29, 91, 92
civil servants, 42
Civil War, 116
clarity, 60

classes, 6, 9
collateral, 23, 27, 119
commerce, 6
commercial, 2, 3, 13, 103
commercial bank, 2, 13
commodity, 72
communication, 7, 66
complement, 4
compliance, 5, 8
composition, 24, 74, 110
conference, ix, 121
conflict, 38, 63
Congress, vii, viii, ix, 1, 2, 5, 7, 8, 9, 11, 12, 13, 14, 21, 26, 27, 28, 29, 33, 34, 37, 42, 44, 45, 46, 47, 48, 55, 57, 58, 59, 65, 66, 67, 74, 75, 78, 79, 80, 83, 85, 86, 93, 95, 100, 112, 116, 119, 121, 125
Congressional Budget Office, 48
consensus, 21, 46, 100, 102, 115
consent, 1, 2, 9, 36
Constitution, 27, 34, 53
construction, 5, 17
consumer goods, 70, 77, 86
consumer price index, 61, 72, 86, 91, 102
consumer protection, 73, 74
Consumer Protection Act, vii, ix, 2, 9, 10, 14, 26, 30, 73, 74, 82, 121
consumers, 6, 13, 74, 101, 114
consumption, 38, 81, 87, 88, 114, 118
cooperation, 126
coordination, 21, 34, 35, 41, 45, 46, 51, 124, 126, 129
core inflation, viii, 61, 62, 72, 78, 80, 85, 86, 87, 88, 89, 90, 91, 92
cost, vii, 11, 13, 14, 15, 38, 43, 46, 76, 112
CPI, 61, 65, 72, 76, 77, 81, 86, 87, 88, 90, 117
credit market, 71, 106
crises, 14
criticism, 28, 43, 50, 56, 63, 66, 68, 69, 72, 80, 111
crowding out, 30, 39
crowds, 20, 39

CRS report, 52
currency, 6, 14, 15, 25, 35, 37, 82, 95
customers, 5
cycles, 17, 34, 41, 43, 61

D

danger, 16
data mining, 91
database, 82
debt service, 112
deficit, 18, 19, 20, 39, 40, 45, 94, 95, 108, 111, 112, 113
deflation, 34, 42, 53, 56, 61, 69, 70, 71, 75, 76, 81, 101, 102, 108
deflator, 77, 81, 87
delegates, 5
delinquency, 22
democracy, viii, 33, 34, 47
depository financial institutions, vii, 1, 6
depository institutions, 4, 13, 14, 15, 16, 22
deposits, 4, 11, 14, 15, 16, 97, 110
depreciation, 17
depth, 10, 56, 57, 80, 82
derivatives, 129
detection, 123
developed countries, 17
deviation, 77, 87
directives, vii, 4, 11, 13
directors, 5, 6, 9
disclosure, 7, 9, 27, 47, 48
discretionary policy, 34, 44, 50
discrimination, 123
disposable income, 39
distress, 125, 129, 130
distribution, 128
divergence, 87
Dodd-Frank Act, ix, 12, 14, 17, 26, 27, 29, 31, 121, 122, 124, 126, 127, 129, 130
Dodd-Frank Wall Street Reform, vii, ix, 2, 9, 10, 14, 26, 30, 73, 74, 82, 121

E

earnings, 6, 128
economic activity, 20, 41, 58, 64, 67, 90, 94, 129
economic consequences, 130
economic crisis, 101
economic development, 64, 75, 128
economic disadvantage, 49
economic downturn, 48, 63
economic efficiency, 47, 62
economic evaluation, 53
economic growth, 24, 30, 40, 49, 65, 71, 90, 101, 102, 114, 115, 126
economic growth rate, 40
economic performance, 29, 65
economic policy, 38, 46
economic power, 34, 44
economic theory, 62, 81, 110
economic welfare, 49
economics, 35, 43, 49
election, 10, 43
emergency, 4, 9, 23, 24, 68, 73, 96, 99, 103, 112, 116
Emergency Economic Stabilization Act, 112, 119
employees, 6
employment, viii, 3, 12, 13, 14, 17, 18, 23, 28, 30, 33, 34, 37, 39, 40, 41, 42, 44, 45, 51, 55, 57, 60, 61, 62, 63, 64, 70, 71, 76, 80, 93, 95, 100, 101, 102, 104, 114, 115
employment growth, 60, 114
energy, viii, 28, 61, 72, 78, 85, 86, 87, 88, 89, 90, 91, 92
energy price volatility, viii, 85
energy prices, viii, 61, 78, 85, 86, 87, 89, 90
England, 50, 125
environment, ix, 75, 103, 122
equilibrium, 20, 82
equipment, 12, 17, 38, 106
equity, 20, 101
EU, 125
Europe, 83, 101, 128

Index

European Union, 125
evidence, 25, 40, 43, 48, 61, 67, 90, 104, 106, 107, 114
evolution, 123
examinations, 5, 6
exchange rate, 17, 38, 39, 45, 49, 53, 108, 109, 118
execution, 29
executive branch, 34, 42, 43, 67
exercise, 34, 127
expenditures, 5, 6, 81, 87, 88
exports, 17, 20, 38, 39, 94, 108, 115
exposure, 112

F

Fair Housing Act, 5
faith, 52
false positive, 72
fear, 25, 34, 67, 71, 100, 102, 107, 117, 118
federal agency, 4, 79
federal funds, ix, 4, 12, 15, 16, 21, 22, 23, 24, 29, 30, 37, 58, 69, 93, 95, 96, 102, 105, 108, 112, 114
federal government, vii, 1, 2, 6, 7, 37, 44, 112, 113
Federal Reserve Banks, vii, 1, 2, 5, 6, 7, 36, 37
Federal Reserve Board, 5, 9, 10, 116, 117, 118, 119, 125
Federal Reserve System, iv, vi, vii, viii, 1, 2, 3, 4, 5, 7, 9, 10, 25, 29, 31, 33, 34, 35, 36, 52, 57, 121
financial, vii, viii, ix, 1, 2, 3, 4, 5, 6, 7, 9, 10, 11, 12, 13, 14, 16, 17, 21, 22, 23, 25, 26, 29, 30, 31, 35, 56, 57, 58, 61, 65, 68, 69, 70, 72, 73, 74, 79, 80, 82, 90, 94, 96, 97, 99, 101, 103, 106, 107, 108, 110, 114, 121, 122, 123, 124, 125, 126, 127, 128, 129, 130
financial condition, 12, 23, 25, 99, 103, 106
financial crisis, viii, ix, 4, 9, 10, 11, 12, 13, 14, 17, 21, 22, 26, 29, 30, 31, 57, 58, 61, 65, 68, 70, 73, 82, 97, 101, 107, 108, 114, 121, 130
financial data, 124
financial development, 126
financial distress, 125, 130
financial instability, 126
financial institutions, vii, 1, 4, 5, 6, 14, 16, 23, 74, 122, 127, 129
financial intermediaries, 14
financial markets, viii, 4, 11, 56, 65, 70, 79, 90, 108, 114, 124, 126, 130
financial oversight, ix, 122
financial regulation, 122, 129
financial sector, 22, 68, 69, 110, 122
financial stability, 10, 13, 14, 21, 70, 80, 82, 123, 124, 125, 128, 130
Financial Stability Oversight Council, ix, 9, 82, 122, 124, 125, 126, 128, 131
financial system, viii, ix, 3, 4, 11, 12, 13, 14, 22, 23, 35, 69, 72, 80, 82, 94, 96, 97, 101, 103, 121, 122, 124, 125, 127, 128, 129
fiscal deficit, 45
fiscal policy, 18, 19, 20, 21, 30, 33, 34, 35, 36, 39, 40, 41, 42, 44, 45, 46, 51, 53
flexibility, 28, 50, 59, 60, 75, 79
flight, 109
fluctuations, 47, 90
food, viii, 61, 72, 78, 85, 86, 87, 88, 89, 91, 92
force, 48, 111
forecasting, 78, 90, 92, 103
foreign banks, 5, 73
foreign capital flows, 20
foreign firms, 74
foreign investment, 39
fragility, 110
friction, 109
fruits, 91
full employment, 18, 30, 39, 40, 41, 63, 76, 101, 102, 104, 115
funding, viii, 33, 34, 42, 123, 126, 127, 129

funds, ix, 4, 6, 12, 15, 16, 19, 22, 23, 24, 29, 30, 37, 58, 69, 83, 93, 94, 95, 96, 98, 102, 105, 108, 112, 114, 126

G

GAO, 7, 9, 10, 12, 14, 26, 47, 53
GDP, 17, 18, 30, 77, 81, 87, 88, 101, 103, 113, 117
GDP deflator, 77, 87
General Accounting Office, 7
Georgia, 82, 83
goods and services, 39, 86, 87
government securities, 2, 4, 6
governments, 13, 113
governor, 3
grants, 27, 34
Great Depression, 23, 35, 38, 68, 114, 116, 117
Great Recession, 117
gross domestic product, 81, 87, 100
growth, vii, ix, 11, 15, 17, 18, 24, 25, 30, 37, 40, 49, 50, 57, 58, 60, 65, 69, 71, 74, 88, 89, 90, 93, 95, 96, 101, 103, 104, 105, 109, 111, 114, 115, 116, 126
growth rate, 40, 49, 89, 101, 109
guessing, 47
guidance, 59, 63

H

health, 127
height, 126
history, 7, 13, 17, 75
holding company, 6
homes, 38
House, 26, 61, 81, 118, 119
House of Representatives, 118
household income, 88
housing, 13, 17, 22, 30, 56, 57, 69, 70, 71, 73, 74, 80, 82, 94, 108, 110, 116
hyperinflation, 18, 40

hypothesis, 69
hysteresis, 63

I

identification, 125
identity, 9
idiosyncratic, 47
illusion, 76
imbalances, 40, 45, 108
imports, 17, 20, 108
income, 2, 6, 20, 29, 37, 39, 88, 94, 111, 112
incompatibility, 36
independence, viii, 2, 7, 21, 27, 28, 29, 33, 34, 35, 37, 42, 43, 44, 46, 47, 48, 49, 51, 52, 56, 59, 62, 65, 67, 79, 108
Independence, 27, 30, 31, 33, 41, 42, 53
individuals, 41, 62, 82, 86
industry, 6, 8, 126, 127
inflation, viii, 12, 15, 16, 17, 18, 25, 28, 29, 30, 31, 33, 34, 38, 40, 41, 42, 43, 44, 45, 49, 50, 51, 52, 53, 55, 56, 57, 58, 59, 60, 61, 62, 63, 64, 65, 66, 67, 68, 69, 70, 71, 72, 74, 75, 76, 77, 78, 79, 80, 81, 82, 85, 86, 87, 88, 89, 90, 91, 92, 93, 94, 95, 100, 101, 102, 105, 109, 110, 111, 114, 115, 117
inflation target, viii, 28, 50, 52, 53, 55, 56, 57, 58, 59, 60, 61, 62, 65, 66, 68, 69, 72, 74, 75, 76, 77, 79, 80, 81, 82
information sharing, 124
inspections, 6
institutions, vii, 1, 4, 5, 6, 14, 15, 16, 22, 23, 24, 29, 31, 43, 74, 97, 116, 117, 122, 123, 124, 126, 127, 129, 130
insulation, 43
integrity, 26
interest rates, viii, 3, 12, 13, 15, 16, 17, 19, 20, 21, 22, 23, 25, 28, 33, 35, 37, 38, 39, 40, 42, 45, 46, 49, 50, 51, 55, 57, 66, 67, 68, 69, 72, 76, 86, 89, 90, 94, 95, 101,

102, 104, 106, 107, 108, 111, 112, 114, 116, 117, 119
intermediaries, 14
internal controls, 26
International Monetary Fund, 82, 83, 117
internationalization, 17
intervention, 13
investment, 12, 17, 20, 38, 39, 40, 94, 106, 109, 114, 127
investment rate, 109
investors, 15, 20, 74, 75, 83, 106, 108, 109, 111, 113, 119
isolation, 21, 30, 33, 41, 45, 65, 79
issues, 8, 14, 26, 52, 56, 66, 74, 77, 118

J

Japan, 95, 101, 115, 117, 118, 119
job creation, 126
jobless, 69
judicial branch, 42
jurisdiction, 58, 125
justification, 58, 60

L

labor market, 62, 76
landscape, 124
laws, 5
lead, 20, 28, 38, 40, 50, 67, 70, 76, 78, 79, 80, 90, 98, 101, 104, 105, 106, 107, 112, 114, 115, 126, 129
leadership, 3, 10, 127
Leahy, 119
legislation, ix, 5, 19, 37, 59, 65, 119, 122
legislative authority, 38
lender of last resort, vii, 3, 11, 13, 14, 58, 68, 82, 103
lending, 4, 9, 12, 13, 14, 15, 16, 17, 22, 23, 24, 25, 26, 27, 29, 37, 58, 68, 71, 73, 94, 96, 97, 98, 99, 103, 104, 105, 109, 110, 114, 115, 116, 117, 119, 123

liberty, 51
light, 65, 71, 82
liquidity, viii, 4, 11, 12, 15, 22, 23, 25, 29, 31, 37, 68, 73, 74, 94, 96, 97, 101, 103, 104, 107, 110, 111, 114, 127, 129
liquidity trap, 25, 101
loans, 7, 9, 12, 14, 15, 16, 22, 23, 24, 27, 96, 97, 99, 104, 108, 112, 114

M

macroeconomic models, 108, 114
macroeconomic policy, viii, 33, 35, 61, 85
magnitude, 23, 41, 103
majority, 23
management, 14, 41, 46, 53, 126, 127, 128
manipulation, 91
market discipline, 82, 124
market participants, vii, 11, 65, 66, 67, 129
matter, iv, 8, 18, 25, 43, 63
measurements, 91
median, 92
membership, ix, 122, 124, 127
Minneapolis, 6
Missouri, 83
models, 48, 108, 109, 114, 128
momentum, 22
monetary expansion, 40, 118
monetary policy instruments, 4
money illusion, 76
money supply, 25, 36, 39, 40, 42, 49, 94, 96, 98, 104, 105, 109, 110, 114, 115, 116, 117, 123, 129
moral hazard, 73
mortgage-backed securities, ix, 24, 68, 71, 93, 95, 99
multinational firms, 129
multiplier, 19, 104, 105, 114

N

national income, 20

natural rate of unemployment, 63, 82
negative effects, 51
net exports, 115
neutral, 15, 18, 21, 62, 63, 64, 108
New Zealand, 58, 61, 83
No Child Left Behind, 53
Norway, 119

O

Office of Management and Budget, 48
officials, 30, 36, 42, 43, 47, 48, 49, 51, 52, 66, 67, 106, 119
oil, 50, 64, 79, 89, 91
open market operations, 3, 4, 6, 11, 12, 15, 17, 20, 21, 23, 27, 28, 36, 37, 63, 113
openness, 20
operating costs, 37
operational independence, 27
operations, vii, 1, 2, 3, 4, 5, 6, 7, 8, 9, 11, 12, 15, 17, 20, 21, 23, 27, 28, 36, 37, 46, 63, 110, 111, 113, 119, 130
opportunities, 104, 129
oversight, vii, ix, 1, 2, 5, 7, 8, 9, 12, 13, 14, 26, 27, 28, 29, 35, 47, 48, 49, 51, 52, 56, 58, 66, 122, 123, 124, 125, 127, 129, 130

P

pain, 43, 51
participants, vii, 11, 65, 66, 67, 124, 129
penalties, 56, 75, 78, 79
Philadelphia, 6, 29, 30
playing, 100, 129
polar, 50
policy initiative, 68
policy instruments, 4, 130
policy options, 3, 21, 65
policy rate, 69
policymakers, viii, 19, 20, 21, 27, 34, 41, 61, 64, 65, 70, 74, 75, 76, 79, 81, 85, 86, 87, 88, 89, 91, 124

poor performance, 64
portfolio, 4, 15, 16, 36, 37, 96, 104, 106
potential benefits, 51, 126
predictability, 56
preparation, 43
president, 3, 6, 31, 36
President, 1, 2, 3, 9, 16, 27, 36, 45, 46, 67, 131
prevention, 123
price changes, 75, 78, 86, 89, 90
price deflator, 87
price effect, 40, 41
price index, 61, 72, 75, 76, 77, 86, 102
price signals, 86
price stability, viii, 12, 14, 17, 28, 30, 31, 55, 56, 57, 59, 60, 61, 62, 63, 64, 67, 70, 71, 72, 75, 79, 80, 81, 86, 100, 102
private investment, 20
profit, 7, 111
profitability, 8
proposition, 76
protection, 73, 74, 123
prudential regulation, 125
public opinion, 42, 43
purchasing power, 76, 86, 88

Q

quantitative easing, ix, 12, 24, 25, 56, 57, 68, 70, 71, 81, 83, 93, 94, 95, 96, 101, 102, 103, 104, 105, 108, 111, 114, 115, 116, 118, 119

R

rate of return, 20
rational expectations, 47, 111
reactions, 64
reading, 48
real estate, 101
real terms, 109
real wage, 76

reality, 78, 109
reasoning, 89
recession, 19, 21, 22, 39, 45, 50, 51, 56, 57, 63, 64, 68, 69, 78, 80, 90, 99, 100, 101, 102, 108, 114, 115, 117
recommendations, iv, 9, 125
recovery, 5, 24, 69, 70, 71, 100, 102, 128
reform, 9, 45, 129
Reform, vii, ix, 2, 8, 9, 10, 14, 26, 30, 31, 37, 52, 57, 73, 74, 82, 121, 129
regulations, 5, 8, 125, 128, 129
regulatory agencies, ix, 5, 122, 124, 126, 130
regulatory framework, ix, 47, 121
regulatory requirements, 14
remittances, 111, 112, 113
repo, 103, 119
reputation, 67
requirements, 4, 8, 11, 14, 15, 26, 28, 29, 122, 127, 128, 129, 130
Reserve Bank of New Zealand, 83
reserves, 4, 12, 13, 14, 15, 16, 25, 29, 38, 94, 96, 97, 98, 104, 105, 109, 110, 111, 112, 114, 115, 116, 117, 118, 119
resistance, 109
resolution, 125, 127
resource utilization, 100
resources, 30, 38, 40, 45, 47, 86
response, 4, 10, 12, 14, 18, 19, 25, 28, 35, 41, 63, 65, 78, 89, 107, 108, 123
responsiveness, 44
restrictions, 12, 14, 26, 79, 126
revenue, 30, 37
rewards, 51
risk, ix, 17, 29, 46, 71, 73, 75, 95, 102, 107, 111, 112, 115, 116, 121, 122, 124, 125, 126, 127, 128, 129, 130
risks, ix, 25, 73, 82, 100, 102, 115, 122, 123, 124, 125, 126, 127, 128, 129, 130
root, 65, 73, 101
rules, 29, 34, 47, 48, 49, 50, 51, 52, 53, 126, 129

S

safe haven, 109
safety, 5, 73, 74, 122, 128, 129, 130
savings, 6, 9, 22
scope, 14, 20, 22, 51, 52, 61, 65, 66, 74
Secretary of the Treasury, 131
securities, ix, 2, 4, 6, 11, 12, 13, 15, 16, 23, 24, 25, 36, 37, 68, 71, 83, 93, 94, 95, 96, 99, 100, 104, 106, 107, 108, 109, 110, 112, 113, 114, 116, 117, 118, 119, 125
security, 7, 97, 99, 100, 111
seigniorage, 37
seller, 98
Senate, 1, 2, 9, 26, 36, 81
services, vii, 1, 2, 5, 6, 8, 13, 39, 86, 123
shareholders, 37
shock, 28, 50, 64, 101
shortage, 16
short-term interest rate, 15, 16, 17, 22, 67, 68, 116, 119
side effects, 69
signals, 72, 86
simulations, 82
Social Security, 88
society, 49
solution, 46
specialists, 127
specialization, 66
speculation, 47, 57
speech, 17, 25, 29, 30, 31, 51, 82, 92, 117
spending, 12, 13, 17, 18, 19, 20, 25, 30, 38, 39, 40, 45, 70, 89, 94, 101, 104, 106, 108, 114, 118
spillover effects, 22
spillovers, 129
Spring, 82, 99
stability, viii, ix, 2, 10, 12, 13, 14, 17, 21, 28, 30, 31, 34, 49, 50, 55, 56, 57, 59, 60, 61, 62, 63, 64, 67, 70, 71, 72, 75, 76, 79, 80, 81, 82, 86, 100, 102, 108, 122, 123, 124, 125, 126, 128, 130
stabilization, 19, 35, 39, 44, 46, 86

Index

stagflation, 64, 111
standard deviation, 87
state, ix, 2, 5, 6, 7, 9, 41, 59, 73, 96, 122
states, 35, 125
statutory mandate, viii, 12, 13, 14, 17, 28, 55, 57, 59, 74, 93, 94, 95, 100, 113
stimulus, 20, 21, 23, 25, 30, 56, 68, 94, 96, 99, 100, 101, 102, 103, 104, 105, 108, 115
stockholders, 119
stress, 13, 50, 127, 128
structure, vii, viii, 1, 2, 9, 27, 33, 34, 35, 36, 41, 42, 43, 122, 123, 124, 125, 127
substitutes, 20
supervision, ix, 2, 9, 13, 17, 41, 58, 80, 122, 123, 127, 130
supervisors, 127, 128
supply shock, 64, 89
surplus, 7, 39, 45, 119
sustainability, 13, 37, 128
systemic risk, ix, 17, 122, 124, 126, 127, 130

T

target, viii, 4, 12, 16, 20, 22, 28, 29, 37, 49, 50, 52, 53, 55, 56, 57, 58, 59, 60, 62, 65, 66, 69, 72, 74, 75, 76, 77, 78, 79, 80, 81, 82, 83, 96, 112
tax cuts, 19, 30, 48
taxes, 39, 45
threats, ix, 82, 122, 124, 125, 130
time periods, 88, 89
trade, 20, 38, 39, 46, 108
trade deficit, 20, 108
trading partners, 109
transactions, 2, 4, 8, 9, 23, 27
transmission, 22, 103
transparency, 9, 12, 26, 28, 56, 59, 65, 66, 78, 79, 83
Treasury, ix, 2, 4, 6, 7, 11, 12, 13, 15, 16, 23, 24, 25, 37, 46, 48, 50, 67, 71, 93, 94, 95, 96, 97, 99, 106, 107, 108, 110, 111, 112, 113, 114, 116, 117, 118, 119, 124, 131

U

U.S. economy, 21, 90, 109
U.S. Treasury, 4, 7, 11, 13, 15, 16, 25, 37
underwriting, 74
unemployment insurance, 30
unemployment rate, 82, 100, 101
United, iv, vii, 1, 13, 17, 20, 28, 38, 56, 57, 61, 81, 95, 101, 103, 116, 118, 122, 124, 125, 129
United Kingdom, 58, 62, 125
United States, iv, vii, 1, 13, 17, 20, 28, 38, 56, 57, 61, 81, 95, 101, 103, 116, 118, 122, 124, 125, 129

V

volatility, viii, 65, 78, 85, 87, 90, 91, 129
vote, 3, 4, 9, 36, 48
voting, 124, 131

W

wages, 18, 76, 77, 88
war, ix, 121
Washington, 36, 82, 91, 117, 119
weakness, 90, 101
wealth, 86, 88, 118
welfare, 47, 49
wholesale, 123
workers, 76
working groups, 125, 128
World War I, 75, 100, 101, 113

Y

yield, 67, 105, 107, 111, 118